P9-DES-361

THE PENTATEUCH

INTERPRETING BIBLICAL TEXTS

The Gospels, Fred B. Craddock

New Testament Apocalyptic Literature, Paul S. Minear

The Pentateuch, Lloyd R. Bailey

INTERPRETING **ibt** BIBLICAL TEXTS

The Pentateuch

Lloyd R. Bailey

LLOYD R. BAILEY
and
VICTOR PAUL FURNISH
EDITORS

ABINGDON   NASHVILLE

THE PENTATEUCH

Copyright © 1981 by Abingdon

All rights reserved.
No part of this book may be reproduced in any manner whatsoever without written permission of the publisher except brief quotations embodied in critical articles or reviews. For information address Abingdon, Nashville, Tennessee.

Library of Congress Cataloging in Publication Data

BAILEY, LLOYD R., 1936–
  The Pentateuch.
  (Interpreting Biblical texts)
  Bibliography: p.
  1. Bible. O.T. Pentateuch—Criticism, interpretation, etc.
  I. Title. II. Series.
  BS1225.2.B3   222'.106   81-4495   AACR2

ISBN 0-687-30610-8

Scripture quotations unless otherwise noted are from the Revised Standard Version of the Bible, copyrighted 1946, 1952, © 1971, 1973 by the Division of Christian Education of the National Council of the Churches of Christ in the U.S.A. Used by permission.

Quotations noted NEB are from The New English Bible © the Delegates of the Oxford University Press and the Syndics of the Cambridge University Press 1961, 1970. Reprinted by permission.

Quotations from the New Scofield Reference Bible and from The Anchor Bible are so indicated; quotations from the King James Version are noted KJV and those from Today's English Version, TEV.

MANUFACTURED BY THE PARTHENON PRESS AT
NASHVILLE, TENNESSEE, UNITED STATES OF AMERICA

The apostle Paul tells us, in his first letter to the church at Corinth, of a love which endures all things and demands nothing in return (13:4-7). This book is for Judith Ann, who has convinced me that that long-dead apostle spoke the truth.

ABBREVIATIONS

ANE: Ancient Near East
HUCA: Hebrew Union College Annual
IDB: Interpreter's Dictionary of the Bible
IDBS: Interpreter's Dictionary of the Bible,
     Supplementary Volume
JB: Jerusalem Bible
KJV: King James Version
NAB: New American Bible
NEB: New English Bible
NIV: New International Version
NJV: New Jewish Version
NT: New Testament
OT: Old Testament
RSV: Revised Standard Version
TEV: Today's English Version

INTERPRETING BIBLICAL TEXTS:
Editors' Foreword

The volumes in this series have been planned for those who are convinced that the Bible has meaning for our life today, and who wish to enhance their skills as interpreters of the biblical texts. Such interpreters must necessarily engage themselves in two closely related tasks: (1) determining as much as possible about the original meaning of the various biblical writings, and (2) determining in what respect these texts are still meaningful today. The objective of the present series is to keep both of these tasks carefully in view, and to provide assistance in relating the one to the other.

Because of this overall objective it would be wrong to regard the individual volumes in this series as commentaries, as homiletical expositions of selected texts, or as abstract discussions of "the hermeneutical problem." Rather, they have been written in order to identify and illustrate what is involved in relating the meaning of the biblical texts in their own times to their meaning in ours. Biblical commentaries and other technical reference works sometimes focus exclusively on the first, paying little or no attention to the second. On the other hand, many attempts to expound the contemporary "relevance" of biblical themes or passages pay scant attention to the intentions of the texts themselves. And although one of the standard topics of "hermeneutics" is how a text's original meaning relates to its present meaning, such discussions often employ highly technical philosophical language and proceed with little reference to concrete examples. By way of contrast, the present volumes are written in language that will be understood by scholars, clergy and laypersons alike, and they deal with concrete texts, actual problems of interpretation, and practical procedures for moving from "then" to "now."

Each contributor to this series is committed to three basic tasks: (1) a description of the salient features of the particular type of biblical literature or section of the canon assigned to him; (2) the identification and explanation of the basic assumptions that guide his analysis and explication of those materials; and (3) the discussion of possible contemporary meanings of representative texts, in view of the specified assumptions with which the interpreter approaches them. Considerations that should be borne in mind by the interpreter in reflecting upon contemporary meanings of these texts are introduced by the sign ● and are accentuated with a different size of type.

The assumptions that are brought to biblical interpretation may vary from one author to the next, and will undoubtedly differ from those of many readers. Nonetheless, we believe that the present series, by illustrating how careful interpreters carry out their tasks, will encourage readers to be more reflective about the way they interpret the Bible.

Lloyd Bailey
Duke Divinity School

Victor Paul Furnish
Perkins School of Theology
Southern Methodist University

CONTENTS

**CHAPTER ONE—THE PAST: THE TEXT
WE MUST INTERPRET**   **13**

   I. What Is the Pentateuch (Torah)?   13
      A. "Torah" Does Not Mean "Law"   14
      B. Pentateuch As Story   16
      C. The Authority of Torah   21
  II. Continuous Story? or Collection
     of Stories?   22
      A. Unity Within the Pentateuch   22
      B. Diversity Within the Pentateuch   23
 III. An Author? or Editors (Collectors)?   26
      A. Single-Author Model:
         Rationale; Problems   26
      B. Documentary-Hypothesis Model:
         Rationale; Description;
         Problems   35
      C. Complex-of-Traditions Model:
         Rationale; Problems   54
      D. From Scroll to Printed Text   59

**CHAPTER TWO—THE BRIDGE BETWEEN
PAST AND PRESENT: THE ASSUMPTIONS
OF THE INTERPRETER**   **61**

   I. Interpretation Is Necessary 61
      A. Lack of Clarity 61
      B. Differences of Opinion 66
  II. The Nature of the Interpreter 67
      A. Impulsive Decisions 67
      B. Personal Needs and
         Preconceived Opinions 69
      C. Identification with the
         Wrong Actors 74
 III. Assumptions About the Bible 75
      A. Bible Study Is a Worthwhile
         Activity 75
      B. The Text Is Scripture 76
      C. Is the Text an Account
         of "What Happened"? 80
      D. Critical Study Is Essential 81
      E. Multiple Points of View
         in the Text 82
      F. The Bible "Speaks in the Language
         of Human Beings" 87
  IV. The Move from Past to Present 89
      A. Subjectivity 89
      B. Continuity 90
      C. Individualization 92
      D. Spiritualization 92
      E. Substitution 94
      F. Humanization 94

**CHAPTER THREE—LEVELS OF MEANING
IN THE TEXT**   **95**

    I. What the Author Actually Said 95
        A. The Literal Meaning
           of the Words 95
        B. The Meaning of the Words
           in Context 101
        C. The Overall Meaning of
           a Literary Unit 103
   II. What the Author Meant to Say 107
  III. What the Author Intended
        to Accomplish 109
  IV. What the Audience Understood 112
   V. What the Editor (Redactor) Meant 114
  VI. What Later Generations Within
        the Old Testament Understood 115
 VII. New Testament Reinterpretation 117
VIII. Traditional Understandings in
        Other Than Canonical Literature 119
  IX. What the Text Means
        to the Modern Reader 121

**CHAPTER FOUR—THE PRESENT: POSSIBLE
APPLICATION OF SELECTED TEXTS**   **125**

    I. The Creation Account
       —Genesis 1:1–2:4a 126
   II. The Bridge Between the Primeval
       and the Patriarchal
       —Genesis 12 132
  III. The Naming of Isaac
       —Genesis 17:15-22; 18:1-16; 21:1-7 142
  IV. The Near-Sacrifice of Isaac
       —Genesis 22 146

V. The Ten Commandments
—Exodus 20:1-17   150
VI. The Necessity for Tassels on Garments
—Numbers 15:37-41   155

AIDS FOR THE INTERPRETER   159

THE PAST: THE TEXT
WE MUST INTERPRET

CHAPTER ONE

I. What Is the Pentateuch (Torah)?

The use of the term "Pentateuch" to describe the first five books of the Bible goes back at least to the Church Father Tertullian (second century A.D.). It is a two-part Greek word: *penta* (five), plus *teuchos* (scroll).[1] Therefore he speaks of the *pentateuchos biblios,* the "five-scrolled book." A similar designation is attested slightly later in Jewish sources, where each scroll is regarded as one-fifth of Moses' work; the totality often was called the five-fifths of the Torah.

The first scroll covers events from creation through the time of Israel's "founding fathers" (the Patriarchs), and its name, Genesis, comes from the Greek word meaning "beginning."[2] The second scroll relates Israel's

[1]That the OT texts traditionally were written on scrolls (prepared animal skins) will be clear to anyone who has heard of the Dead Sea Scrolls (see the *IDB* article by that title, with photos). The word *teuchos* seems to mean, basically, "jar." Whether this is related to the practice of storing scrolls in ceramic jars (as at Qumran, where the Dead Sea Scrolls were found) is unclear.

[2]The title of each of the first five books, as commonly printed in English Bibles, goes back to the Greek (early Christian) Bible. The

13

experience in Egyptian bondage and her "going out" from there (Greek: *ex-odos*).[3] The third section is concerned largely with the duties of the Levitical priests and hence is called Leviticus.[4] The fourth is called Numbers, since it contains several enumerations of Israel's population.[5] And the last is Deuteronomy ("repetition of the Torah"), because Moses, depicted as standing on the border of the land of Canaan, reminds Israel of her identity and obligations.[6]

A. *"Torah" Does Not Mean "Law"*

While modern scholars have adopted Tertullian's designation (Pentateuch) for the first five books of the OT, the Church at large has not been familiar with it and has preferred to refer to this material as "law." Indeed, English translations of both the relevant Hebrew *(torah)* and Greek *(nomos)* terms reflect this point of view: "When Moses commanded us a law *(torah)* (Deut 33:4 RSV); "For the law *(nomos)* was given through Moses" (John 1:17 RSV). Under the impression that such translations are accurate and that the intent of the material is to judge and condemn, the Church often has

---

Hebrew titles, by contrast, are derived from the first few words of the text itself, in accordance with ANE custom. That of Gen., therefore, is *berēshīt* ("In the beginning").

[3]The Hebrew title: "And These Are the Names" *(we'ēlleh shemōt)*.

[4]The Hebrew title: "And He Called" *(wayyiqra')*.

[5]The Hebrew title is a more accurate summary of the scroll's contents: "In the Wilderness" *(bemidbā*r); also called "And He Spoke" (wayedabbēr).

[6]The Hebrew title: "These Are the Words" *('ēlleh haddebārīm)*.

compared it unfavorably with the NT, perhaps taking its lead from St. Paul: "For God has done what the law *(nomos)* . . . could not do: sending his own son" (Rom 8:3 RSV); "Law *(nomos)* came in, to increase the trespass" (Rom 5:20 RSV).

The Church frequently has used "law" to characterize not only these first five books, but the entire OT. It has been set in contrast to the NT, which is characterized as "gospel" (that is, "the good news"). This negative comparison is reflected not only in overt polemics but *de facto,* in the tradition of standing during Christian worship to hear "the Gospel" read; in the fact that the vast majority of sermons are preached from NT texts, despite the fact that the OT comprises four-fifths of the Bible; and in the printing of the NT alone or with only the Psalms, as if the rest were superfluous.[7]

How adequate is the Church's characterization of the OT and of the Pentateuch, in particular, as "law"?

Actual laws comprise only a small percentage of the total text: none of Genesis, part of Exodus, much of Leviticus, a little of Numbers, and really only a part of Deuteronomy (which is largely sermonic). Once we move beyond the Pentateuch to the remainder of the OT, the percentage is practically zero. Is it therefore accurate to characterize the whole by a small part?

The terms torah *and* nomos *do not necessarily mean "law" in the narrow sense.* They are terms for which there is no exact English equivalent; they refer to

[7]E.g., R. E. Sleeth et al., *Proclamation: Aids for Interpreting the Lessons of the Church Year,* series B, "Epiphany" (Philadelphia: Fortress Press, 1975), p. 55, speaks of those "whose hearts are veiled with the old law."

aspects of (sacred) story, teaching, and revelation.[8] Perhaps it would not be overly simplistic to say that the Bible, as Torah, is God's story, which reveals the divine initiatives and teaches the appropriate response.[9]

Those who preserved this material did not think of it as a burden, nor does Judaism to this day. Rather, it is regarded as a source of joy.[10]

B. Pentateuch As Story

Modern readers tend to view the Bible in one of at least three ways.

The antiquarian approach sees the Bible primarily as a window through which one can look at Israel's past—that is, as basically a record of "what happened." It is a source, like any other ancient document, which helps us reconstruct historic events.

Opinions vary as to how much of the Bible can be used reliably in this fashion. Some think that an accurate report of "what happened" begins in Genesis 1:1, or even that we can calculate the very day that creation-out-of-nothing happened.[11] Others propose that more reliable history begins at the transition from the

[8]See especially "Torah," *IDBS,* and the citation of the study by L. M. Pasinya.

[9]In the synagogue, Torah par excellence is the Pentateuch. But the term may be used for the entirety of the (Hebrew) Bible, for its most authoritative updating (Talmud), and for the opinions of the rabbinic authorities.

[10]See "Simhat Torah," *Encyclopaedia Judaica* (1971), vol. 14.

[11]One might consult, as an example, the notes in the New Scofield Reference Bible (New York: Oxford University Press, 1967). Many readers will be familiar with the biblical chronology worked out by the Irish Archbishop James Ussher (1581–1656), who reckoned that creation had begun in 4004 B.C., giving month, day, and hour.

primeval history (Gen 1–11) to the patriarchal stories.[12] The manners and customs, as reported in Genesis 12–50, seem to have parallels in other ancient documents.[13] Still others believe that it is only from the time of the monarchy (Saul and David) downward (roughly 1000 B.C.) that we have reliable documentation.[14] And there are always those who remind us that there is no such thing as "pure" history, either ancient or modern: Any report will involve the values, selectivity, and limited perspective of the writer. The modern interpreter may or may not assume that the biblical writers fall into this category; or that the Bible was or was not intended to tell us "what actually happened," to the satisfaction of clinical historians. If, for example, the famous Greek historian Thucydides, chronicler of the Peloponnesian war, had been standing on the shore of the "Red" Sea, would he have described Israel's escape from Pharaoh in the same way the author of Exodus has done?[15]

There is also a crystal-ball approach to the Bible, which uses it primarily as a window through which to view the future. The prophetic and apocalyptic books in particular are seen by some to contain information about the end of the world. Opinions differ, however, about the proper

[12]This view was popularized by the American archaeologist W. F. Albright during the first half of the 20th century. See "Patriarchs," *IDB*.

[13]See especially the articles "Nuzi" and "Mari," *IDB*. For cautions, see "Patriarch" and "Mari," *IDBS*.

[14]Hence Martin Noth begins his *History of Israel* (New York: Harper & Row, 1960) at the point of settlement in the land.

[15]"Red" is in quotes because there is controversy as to the exact body of water denoted by the Hebrew term *yam suph*. See "Red Sea," *IDB*. I first heard this example of preconceived notions from T. H. Gaster of Columbia University.

way to interpret such literature. The predominant stance of biblical scholars in the present is to see such books as an announcement of God's activity to the author's own situation.

Again, the Bible may be viewed, not as a window to past or future, but as a mirror in which we see our own experience reflected.[16] And this is true, not because the Bible is a prediction of our time, but because it has "photographed" Israel's continuing condition. Each succeeding generation heard the biblical stories and found in them insight into their own situation. A modern writer has stated this function of literature very nicely: "A great story is about everyone, or it will not last. The strange and foreign is not interesting—only the deeply personal and familiar. . . . No story has power, nor will it last, unless we feel in ourselves that it is true and true for us" (John Steinbeck, *East of Eden,* on Gen 4).

I propose therefore that it is helpful to view much of the Bible as "story." This is especially true of the books we will study in this volume (Gen–Deut), and it is true of Genesis 1–11 in particular.

We begin by reminding ourselves that every individual has a "story." Our story tells us how we began, who we are, and it may suggest the values to which our lives should be dedicated. Some are interested in genealogy because it helps them to expand and to deepen their story: It gives them "roots." Some people want to keep a certain parcel of land because it has been in their family for generations: It is part of their story, their self-image, their identity; and it is where their ancestors are buried. Similarly, some try to carry on the traditions and the

[16]I owe this expression to my former colleague, James Sanders. See his "Hermeneutics," *IDBS.*

values that have characterized their ancestors. That is why parents sometimes say to children, "Remember who you are!"

Similarly, a community or a group may have a story about its beginnings, its rules for behavior, its accomplishments, its goals. For many Americans, the national story may begin with ancestral migration to the New World in order to escape the tyranny of a European king or church; it may recall the war for independence (the terrible winter at Valley Forge, etc.); it may include the struggle for the preservation of the Union ("Fourscore and seven years ago . . ."); there is also the Great Depression and its aftermath ("We have nothing to fear but fear itself."); and it might even include the recent rebirth of idealism ("Ask not what your country can do for you . . .").

The story, whether that of an individual or of a group, does at least two things: (a) It gives identity: It answers the question, Who am I? (b) It challenges or sustains identity in moments of crisis. Thus the "story" is retold in order to give direction at crucial moments.

Such an understanding of the Bible is clear in this "Introduction" to Genesis:

> Gen. 12–50 relates Israel's belief that God has chosen the clan of Abraham as an instrument for the rehabilitation of mankind. ["Through you all the families of the earth will be blessed."] Yet, for a variety of reasons . . . the divine promise was not immediately realized. Even the existence of the next generation was often uncertain. [Abraham is 100 years old, and Isaac is not yet born.] And as Genesis concludes, the family has been delivered from famine through divine providence, only to become enslaved in Egypt.

When succeeding generations heard this part of their
story . . . they were enabled to understand that the crises
of the present were not unique, and were able to hope
that the ancient promise would yet be realized.[17]

When we realize that the oldest term for the Bible
(torah) means "story," we need to pause and remind
ourselves that the English word "story" has at least two
meanings: (a) It may mean an untruth, as when we say
to a child, "Now don't tell me a story about what
you've done"; (b) It is a type of literature which may or
may not be historical, but which nonetheless can be
used to "tell the truth." Even Aesop's fables, which
have no historical basis, can convey obvious truths
about human nature! They usually conclude with some
such remark as, "Now, the moral of the story is . . ."
Similarly, the "Bible as Story" is a way of telling the
truth: How God was perceived as acting on behalf of
Israel in the past, and how the people should act in
return. Thus, Torah, as Story, reveals God's initiative
and teaches the appropriate response. This is made
quite clear in Exodus 20, when God is depicted as
directly addressing Israel at Sinai: "I am the Lord your
God, who brought you out of the land of Egypt. . . .
You shall have no other gods before me." Note the
sequence! God's gracious initiative precedes any
response by Israel! Thus ethical guidelines such as the
Ten Commandments (so-called law) are a response,
not a demand! The two are complements, not
opposites.[18]

[17]NEB, Oxford Study Ed. Article written by Lloyd R. Bailey, Sr.;
here slightly adapted and expanded.
[18]See "Grace in the OT," *IDBS.*

C. The Authority of Torah

Why were some of ancient Israel's stories, but not others, preserved in the Bible? It must contain but a small fraction of the stories that were told about Abraham, alone. What accounts for the fact that we have only these particular stories in Genesis?

My assumption is that the community preserved those stories that were useful and that it forgot those that were not. That is, some stories gave the community "staying power": They enabled the group to survive the difficult moments of history. They were a "mirror" in which the succeeding generations could see their own identity reflected, their failures outlined, their hopes reaffirmed. It may have been this kind of story, and this kind alone, that was repeated, handed down to the next generation, treasured, and used liturgically. And that is how they became canonical—that is, in the Bible. The "authority" of the Bible is related to the fact that it had enabled the community to survive.

But with the passage of time, two additional reasons seem to have been given for the "authority" of the biblical books—reasons which now usually are accepted as the basic ones. But they are after-the-fact justifications, and not as profound as the older one.

The stories later were revered and were said to have been placed in the Bible because they were written by an illustrious person. For example, the book of Ecclesiastes was assigned by tradition to Solomon, and the book of Lamentations to Jeremiah.

The stories were revered even later and thought to have been placed in the Bible solely because they were "inspired." In this view, God intended certain material to be Scripture, and it may have been recognized as such from the beginning. Or at least, God later revealed to the community which material should be set aside for Scripture. In any case, in this view, the authority of the material rests largely on the view of its "divine" origin.

II. Continuous Story? or Collection of Stories?

Most of the books with which we are familiar result from one of two processes. On the one hand, there is an "author model," in which a single individual, as the result of creative genius, writes a unified work from beginning to end. The wording is that of the author, except for quotations from earlier publications. Generally we expect the same style throughout, allowing for variations in style and vocabulary which the author may place in the mouths of the characters. Furthermore, we expect the work to be free of contradictions.

On the other hand, there is an "editor model," in which short works by several authors have been collected and placed in sequence. They may be diverse in style and vocabulary and usually represent many individual points of view.

A. Unity Within the Pentateuch

Whatever diversity some people may perceive in this section of the Bible, an overall unity is present. (a) It has been given a separate title and set apart from other canonical divisions—as the "Pentateuch of Moses"; as "Torah," par excellence. (b) It has a distinct beginning (the creation of the world) and end (at the death of Moses). (c) The story moves with dramatic effect and with continuity from one episode to the next. Promises are given to the Patriarchs, and there is a struggle for their realization. The major characters usually are related genealogically, and there is transition from one to the next.

B. Diversity Within the Pentateuch

However well the material tells a continuous story and however well it may have been integrated, the Pentateuch contains a vast number of literary types and styles of writing.

Prose. There are *reports of speeches or prayers* (such as Deut 1:6–4:40, wherein Moses exhorts the people of Israel as they stand at the shore of the Jordan).

There are *public records:* (a) genealogies (e.g., Gen 36:9-14, the descendants of Esau. Interestingly, note the partial overlap with 36:1-5, which raises questions about the preservation and the later consolidation of the material. Is this suggestive of an author model, or of an editor model?); (b) lists (for example, Gen 36:31-39, the kings of Edom; Exod 35:21-29, offerings brought to the tent of meeting by Israel in the wilderness; Num 33, stages of Israel's journey through the wilderness. What person or group would have preserved such diverse data? Always the same one?); (c) regulations governing daily life (Exod 20:22–23:19 seems to be made up of smaller collections of material. Curiously, it seems to presuppose settled agricultural life in Canaan since it mentions fields and vineyards; yet the code is said to have been given earlier at Mt. Sinai. Have later codes of law been incorporated into the Sinai material, as if the entirety had been given there? That is, has the code grown over the generations, as modern codes do?); (d) covenant ceremonies (note Exod 19, in which Israel agrees to accept the

Commandments as an expression of the significance of becoming the people of Yahweh).

There are *narratives:* (a) mythic allusions (e.g., Gen 6:1-4, in which the "sons of God" have intercourse with "daughters of men");[19] (b) tribal sagas (e.g., Gen 25:21-26, which explains, in biological terms, the relationship between the Israelites [Jacob] and the Edomites [Esau]);[20] (c) hero sagas (including Exod 17:8-16, where Moses' role in the defeat of the Amelikites is recorded. At various places in the Pentateuch, there are brief accounts of the exploits of other figures. Did their admirers or their descendants preserve such materials independently?); (d) sanctuary legends (such as Gen 28:10-22, which relates that Jacob, after his dream at Bethel, set up an altar. Thus it would seem to be the account of the first temple on that spot. Who would preserve such an account? The priests? And what are we to make of the fact that excavations at Bethel have shown that a Canaanite city existed there, probably with a temple, long before the time of Jacob? Does this mean that, for Israel, the "relevant" history starts with its own ancestor? Would the Canaanites not have had their own sanctuary legend? What would this imply about the strict historical accuracy of the story?); (e) cultic legends (for example, Gen 17:9-14, which connects the Israelite custom of circumcision with a covenant first made with Abraham. Interestingly,

[19]Few terms in religion have a more flexible definition than the term "myth," and few are more subject to misunderstanding and hostility among persons who are unfamiliar with its meaning. I use it here in the narrow sense of a story (Greek: *muthos*) about the gods.

[20]The terms "saga" and "legend" may not be strictly accurate when applied to biblical literature, having originated in discussion of nonbiblical literature. See "Legend" and "Miracle," *IDB.*

another story [Exod 4:24-26] may suggest that the custom had its origin at the time of Moses. Why would multiple accounts of a custom's origin be preserved if all accounts were written by the same author?); (f) etiologies (These were originally entertaining folk stories which sought to explain the origin of some custom or physical object. Because a remote ancestor did so-and-so, Israel still is said to do it; or the object still is in existence: Why must we work for a living? Because primeval humans caused the ground to be cursed . . . and it still is [Gen 3:17-19]. Why is childbirth painful? Because primeval woman disobeyed God [Gen 3:16]. Why do metallurgists have a strange mark on their forehead? Because the original Mr. Metallurgist [Hebrew: *Qayin*; English "Cain"] wore it as a sign of divine protection [Gen 4:15]. Why do we not eat the sinew from the hip? Because Jacob was wounded there in his wrestling with a divine figure [Gen 32:32]).

Poetry. There are *priestly blessings* (for example, Num 6:24-26, used by Aaron to bless the people in the wilderness); *victory songs* (e.g., Exod 15:1-18 and 15:21, attributed to Moses and Miriam in celebration of the escape from Egypt); *work songs* (such as Num 21:17-18, composed in celebration of a well in the wilderness); *cultic chants* (e.g., Gen 2:23, perhaps part of ancient celebrations of marriage); *family blessings* (note Gen 26:60, attributed to Rebekah's family as she set out to become the wife of Isaac); *clan boasts* (for example, Gen 4:23, where the Lamechites boast that an injury to one of their members will bring seventy sevenfold retribution); *campaign or migration chants* (Exod 17:16 is to be recited during war with the Amelikites; Num 10:35-36,

when Israel sets out daily during the wilderness
journey); *legal pronouncements* (such as Gen 9:6, which
sets the penalty for bloodshed); *blessings and curses* (in
Gen 27:27-29, 39-40, the fortunes of Israel [Jacob] and
Edom [Esau] are outlined in their father's blessing; in
Gen 49, the status of each of the tribes is attributed to a
blessing by their mutual ancestor, Jacob).

III. An Author? or Editors (Collectors)?

We have seen that the material within the Pentateuch is
diverse and that there is considerable reason to believe
that its parts are from various times and situations within
Israel's history. How did it reach its present shape? Did
one person assume the major role so that the totality was
finished in a relatively short time? Or did it continue to
grow across many generations?

A. Single-Author Model

This model most commonly attributes authorship of
the entire Pentateuch to Moses and had been the
near-unanimous assumption of both Synagogue and
Church from the turn of the common era to recent times.

Rationale. It is evident that Moses is the major actor in
the material, which stretches through the events
recorded in Exodus—Deuteronomy. He thus would
have been in the best position to record and narrate most
of the events. He would have needed a description of
events prior to his time, either from earlier sources, or as
"revealed" to him by the deity.

We are specifically told that he committed materials
to writing to guide Israel in the future (Exod 24:4; 34:27;
Num 33:2).

The Pentateuchal materials conclude with the death of Moses (Deut 24).

Elsewhere in the OT, reference is made to "the book of Moses" (Ezra 6:18; Neh 13:1) and to "the book of the law of Moses" (Josh 8:31; 2 Kgs 14:6).

It is hardly surprising, then, that a variety of sources began to attribute authorship of some materials, if not all of the Pentateuch, to Moses (Ben Sirach [Ecclesiasticus 24:23], Philo of Alexandria [*Life of Moses,* 1.4], New Testament writers [Mark 12:26; Acts 15:21], the Jewish historian Josephus [*Antiq* IV.viii.48], and the Talmud [*Bavli, Baba Batra* 14b]).[21]

Modern readers not aware of its inadmissability may propose as another "evidence" of Mosaic authorship the headings before each of the five books. At the beginning of the Pentateuch we find, "The First Book of Moses Commonly Called Genesis" (e.g., KJV and RSV). Thus one would seem to have a direct claim, right in the text itself! Note, however, that the heading is missing in other translations (e.g., NIV, NJV, NAB, JB). It is, in fact, not contained in the original manuscripts, but is an editorial addition by translators, reflecting the traditional assumption of authorship.

Problems. To be sure, there were a few early doubts about Mosaic authorship of the total material, despite the overwhelming concensus. Ezra was credited with reproducing the Mosaic Scriptures which were thought

---

[21]Mark 12:26 is regarded by some modern Christian readers as an especially compelling proof of Mosaic authorship. E.g., the New Scofield Reference Bible, in its preface, "The Pentateuch," states: "Certain critics have denied that Moses wrote Genesis to Deuteronomy despite the fact that they are attributed to Moses by the Lord Jesus Christ."

to have been lost during the Exile (2 Esdr 14); Jerome (fourth cent. A.D.) believed that parts may have been written by Ezra. Some rabbinic sources thought that Joshua wrote about Moses' death at the conclusion of Deuteronomy; but by contrast, Josephus, Philo, and some of the rabbis attributed even this to Moses. Clement of Rome (first cent. A.D.) could not believe that Noah would have been drunk (Gen 9:20ff.) or that he had more than one wife (Gen 25:1), and so he reasoned that Moses could not have written these things, since Moses was not a liar (*Homilies,* II,52; III,55-57)![22] In the second century A.D. Celsus and Ptolemy suggested that all the material could not have been written by one person.[23] In the Middle Ages, Rabbi Ibn Ezra suggested that there might be certain additions to Moses' work, since Genesis 12:6 implies that the Canaanites were no longer in the land at the time of writing, as they certainly were at Moses' time. But such musings were isolated, and there was insufficient knowledge to build a convincing alternative to Mosaic authorship. More than one thousand years would pass before that was possible.

It was the Renaissance period that brought concentrated and systematic attention to pentateuchal studies. Several problems with Mosaic authorship have been perceived since.

Use of Third Person Rather Than First. The text reads "Moses said" or "Moses did," rather than "I said" or "I did."

Different Designations for the Deity. The most

---

[22]This illustrates how the values of the reader can be "read into" the text.

[23]Robert Pfeiffer, *Introduction to the Old Testament* (New York: Harper & Row, 1948), p. 43, n. 2 (citing E. Stein's work).

common designations are "God" and "the Lord."[24] The rabbis had noted this variation long before and suggested that it had to do with the perspective from which the deity was viewed—the former, in his relationship to the entire world; the latter, in his relationship to Israel. This variation led the German Lutheran pastor H. B. Witter (1711) and the French physician Jean Astruc (1753) to suggest that Moses had made use of earlier sources which had used these separate designations. Indeed, the question as to how Moses could have written about the remote ages preceding his own time would need to be answered. The traditional view that God merely had "dictated" the material creates more problems than it solves, since any discrepancy in the text then must be attributed to God rather than to the human author.

Repetitions. We are given the Ten Commandments three times (Exod 20, 34, and Deut 5). A Patriarch gave his wife into the harem of a foreign king on three occasions, asking her to say that she was his sister (Gen 12; 20; 26). The way Isaac received his name, which means "He laughs," is related three times (Gen 17:17; 18:12; 21:6). Note that each account gives a different explanation.

Geographical Discrepancies. Was the Torah given to Moses at Mt. Sinai (Exod 19) or at Mt. Horeb (Deut 1)? Was the tent of meeting, that portable shrine in the wilderness, located completely outside the camp, thus

[24]When English translations use the latter designation, they are substituting it for the proper name of Israel's god, Yahweh, which came to be regarded as too sacred to be pronounced. In general, see *IDB:* "Yahweh," "God, Names of," "Jehovah"; *IDBS:* "Tetragrammaton."

separating it from secular life (Exod 33:7)? Or was it at
the very center, around which all life could be organized
(Num 2:17)?

Chronological Problems. How can Moses refer to a
time "before any king reigned" in Israel (Gen 36:31),
when the monarchy came into existence about 1000 B.C.,
centuries after his lifetime (about 1250 B.C.)? Does not
the statement "At that time the Canaanites were in the
land" (Gen 12:6) imply that it was not so at the time of
the writer? Presumably, then, the writer lived after the
time of Canaanite domination—that is, after David had
defeated them in the tenth century—and thus several
centuries after the time of Moses. How can Moses write
of his own death and also say that no one knows the
place of "his" burial "to this day," since this implies that
it happened long ago (Deut 34:5-6)? How can the
passage continue, "And there has not arisen a prophet
since in Israel like Moses" (v 10)? When did people first
begin to use the divine name Yahweh ("calling upon the
name of the Lord")? Was it at the time of Cain's birth "I
have gotten a man with the help of the Lord" (Gen 4:1)?
Or was it only later, at the time of Enosh—"At that time
men began to call upon the name of the Lord" (Gen
4:26)? Or was it only at the time of Moses—"I appeared
to Abraham . . . as God Almighty, but by my name the
Lord I did not make myself known" (Exod 6:3)?
Contrast such passages as Genesis 15:2, 8, where
Abraham uses the name! How can Moses refer to the
territory of Dan, since this presupposes the settlement
of that tribe in the land at the time of Joshua, after the
death of Moses (Gen 14:14)? How can Moses warn
Israel not to defile the land as did the Canaanites before
them, lest "the land vomit you out . . . as it vomited out

the nation that was before you" (Lev 18:28)? At that time, Israel had not even arrived in the land to cause the "prior nation" to have been "vomited out"!

Variations in Stories. What was the order of creation of humans and animals? Were humans (male and female) created together after all the animals, as the deity's crowning act (Gen 1:24-26)? Or was the male human created first, then all the animals, and then last of all, the human female (Gen 2:18-19)? Who drew Joseph up from the pit and sold him to the Egyptians? Was it the Ishmaelites—"And they took Joseph to Egypt" (Gen 37:25) or was it Midianites—"They drew Joseph up . . . and sold him in Egypt" (vv 28, 36)?

Variations in Language. The grammar and vocabulary of a language change across the centuries, as is evident when wc read *Beowulf* (eighth cent.) or Chaucer (fourteenth cent.) or Carl Sandburg (twentieth cent.). If, however, rather than reading the language "as it was," we read *Beowulf* and Chaucer in a modern English version, they would be less distinguishable from Sandburg, as far as language goes. In just this fashion, the entirety of the Pentateuch, translated as a whole into modern English, disguises the great variety of grammar and syntax that lie behind in the original. Thus it is impossible for the English-language Bible-reader to see that the original contains language characteristics from the tenth century B.C., and from the seventh century, and from the fifth and sixth centuries. How could one author, Moses, have accomplished all that?

Evidence of Once-Independent Units. Note that one could begin reading the Bible at Genesis 5:1 and not realize that anything had preceded or been omitted. We are told that it is the story of Adam, that he was created in God's image, and that he had various descendants. We are told of the birth of Seth (v 3), as if we had not read the other account in 4:25-26. Again, note that chapter 10 begins as a separate unit—"These are the generations" = "This is the story of . . ." It overlaps the information in both chapter 9 and chapter 11.

The modern reader may, of course, be able to "explain" some of these problematic passages (and there are hundreds more) with Moses remaining as author. One must remember, however, that such a reader comes to the text with a preconceived notion, with a certain set of "glasses," since the OT itself does not claim that Moses is the author of all the material in its present form.

"Why be bothered by the third-person style? Maybe it was a custom of the time for a male writer to speak of himself as 'he.'"* On the contrary, the use of the first person was common. The psalmist says, "Answer *me* when *I* call, O God" (4:1); Isaiah remarks, "*I* saw the Lord sitting upon a throne" (6:1); Jeremiah reports, "Now the word of the Lord came to *me*" (4:1); Ezekiel related, "As *I* was among the exiles . . ." (1:1); and Daniel asserts, "As for *me,* Daniel" (7:15) (italics added). There is no reason, then, to assume that Moses would write of himself as "he."

"Why be bothered by variations in what the deity is called? Just as we moderns may speak of God, the Lord, the Almighty, our Father, and so on, in one conversation, why not allow Moses the same freedom?" Granted that such freedom could exist, the problem is much more serious. Such usage often is consistent throughout a

complete story. Thus in a creation account in Genesis 1:1–2:4*a,* the earth is created in six days, followed by a day of rest. The deity, throughout, is called "God," and "God" only. Not once does "the Lord" (Yahweh) make an appearance. Then in 2:4*b,* the account of the Garden of Eden begins and runs through 3:24. With the exception of the conversation with the serpent (3:1-5), the deity consistently is referred to as "the Lord God" (Yahweh-God). In chapter 4, the story of Cain and Abel, the term "the Lord" (Yahweh) is used (excluding the introductory and final verses, which link this account with the stories that come before and after it). Then chapter 5 begins as if chapters 1–4 did not exist—"This is the book of the generations of Adam"—and the deity throughout is referred to as "God." Why is freedom of variation not exercised within the bounds of a story? Why would Moses change only between stories, and not within them? The variations in name, then, remain an interesting, indeed difficult problem for anyone who maintains Mosaic authorship.

"Why be bothered by repetitions? We sometimes repeat ourselves in modern speech. Maybe some things, like the Ten Commandments, were worth hearing more than once, for emphasis! And if Moses gathered documents about events that occurred before his time (as Witter and Astruc thought), could we not expect some duplication and overlap? Maybe he didn't have time to edit his sources to our modern tastes." The problem is that duplicates are found not only in the material Moses might have obtained from earlier sources, but in material *about* Moses! And if the

Commandments are repeated merely for emphasis, why with as many as thirty variations?[25]

"*Why be bothered by geographical discrepancies?* Do we not now use various terms for the same place, such as Chicago, the Windy City, or the Battle of Antietam, the Battle of Sharpsburg? So cannot Sinai and Horeb be alternate names, or two peaks on the same mountain?" True enough! But still a problem remains. Why is there often a consistency of usage within bodies of material? Why does the entire book of Deuteronomy, for example, use only "Horeb"? Why did Moses not mix his designations anywhere in that long series of speeches? Note well! The issue here is not whether there are two mountains rather than one, but whether there are two traditions about its name, in material that Moses should have known best!

"*Why be bothered by chronological problems?* Can't we think of Moses as a prophet who predicted the future and thus could speak of events as if they already had happened?" Perhaps the average reader will agree that this is going pretty far to back up a preconceived notion! In any case, Moses was not considered basically a "prophet" (although he is called that in Deut 34:10), and prophets in ancient Israel were not considered to be basically predictors. Such an interpretation flies in the face of the plain meaning of the text. While it could explain a future-oriented problem (the reference to

[25]The most obvious is that of differing motivations for keeping the sabbath: because God rested after creation (Exod. 20:8-11); or because you remember what it was like in Egypt where there was no rest (Deut. 5:12-14). For a full list of variations, see J. J. Stamm and M. E. Andrew, *The Ten Commandments in Recent Research* (Napierville, Ill.: Allenson, 1967).

kings of Israel in Gen 36:31—kings who lived centuries after Moses), it scarcely can explain a past-oriented one (Canaanites existed in times past, but not during the author's time [Gen 12:6]).

In conclusion, perhaps it is fair to say that Mosaic authorship can be maintained only by the most ingenious efforts and that it need not be seen as a matter of superior "faith" to do so.

B. Documentary-Hypothesis Model[26]

This approach has been the predominant scholarly model for the last two hundred years.

Rationale. There is *great diversity* within the literature, especially that about Moses himself. This seems to suggest a collection of material, rather than authorship. There are *tensions* within the material, especially geographical discrepancies, chronological problems, and differences in subjects. There are *repetitions/doublets.* There is evidence of new beginnings, or *once-independent units,* as if previous stories/chapters did not exist.

Yet there are *limited similarities and continuities,* despite the overall diversities and tensions. That is, a number of stories, self-contained and apparently once independent, nonetheless have similar characteristics, and this may suggest a common origin. When intervening material is ignored, a continuous story may be seen to emerge. Thus two versions of the flood story have been proposed:

[26]The early formulators of this model assumed that the collections began in written (document) form. More recently, oral beginnings have been proposed. See "Tradition, Oral," *IDBS.*

J Account (RSV)

When men began to multiply on the face of the ground
. . . the Lord saw that the wickedness of man was
great. . . . So the Lord said, "I will blot out man. . . ."
But Noah found favor in the eyes of the Lord (Gen 6:1-8).
Then the Lord said to Noah, "Go into the ark." . . . And
Noah did all that the Lord had commanded him (7:1-5).
And Noah and his sons . . . went into the ark. . . . And
after seven days the waters of the flood came upon the
earth (7:7-10). And rain fell upon the earth forty days and
forty nights (7:12). Everything on the dry land . . .
died. . . . Only Noah was left, and those that were with
him in the ark (7:22-23). The rain from the heavens was
restrained, and the waters receded from the earth
continually (8:2b-3a). At the end of forty days . . . Noah
knew that the waters had subsided from the earth. Then
he waited another seven days, and sent forth the dove;
and she did not return to him any more (8:6-12). And
Noah removed the covering of the ark, and looked, and
behold, the face of the ground was dry (8:13b). Then
Noah built an altar to the Lord. . . . And . . . the Lord
said . . . "I will never again . . . destroy every living
creature as I have done" (8:20-22).

P Account (RSV)

These are the generations of Noah . . . Shem, Ham,
and Japheth. Now the earth was corrupt. . . . And God
said to Noah . . . "Make yourself an ark." . . . Noah did
this; he did all that God commanded him (Gen 6:9-22).
Noah was six hundred years old when the flood of waters
came upon the earth (7:6). In the six hundredth year of
Noah's life . . . all the fountains of the great deep burst
forth, and the windows of the heavens were opened
(7:11). On the very same day Noah . . . entered the
ark. . . . The flood continued forty days upon the earth

> . . . And all flesh died . . . and every man (7:13-21). And
> the waters prevailed upon the earth a hundred and fifty
> days. . . . And the waters subsided. . . . The windows of
> the heavens were closed (7:24–8:2a). At the end of a
> hundred and fifty days the waters had abated . . . the ark
> came to rest. . . . The tops of the mountains were seen
> (8:3b-5). In the six hundred and first year . . . the waters
> were dried from off the earth. . . . In the second month
> . . . God said to Noah, "Go forth from the ark." . . . So
> Noah went forth . . . out of the ark (8:14-19).

The J account has characteristics similar to other
stories, such as those about the tower of Babel (Gen
11:1-9) and the Lord's visit with Abraham (Gen 18–19).
The P account has characteristics similar to the
genealogy of Adam (Gen 5) and that of Noah (parts of
Gen 10), as well as the account of the Lord's appearance
to Abraham (Gen 17). Such similarities and continuities
suggested to modern scholars that the Pentateuch
contains a number of individual collections of earlier
stories. The Mosaic model is unable to account for such
diversities and tensions as have been enumerated.

Description. The suggestion of the documentary
hypothesis is that the Pentateuch took its present shape
as the result of four groups of tradition-gathers and
tradition-shapers.

The Yahwists usually use the deity's proper name,
Yahweh. Their collection of material is sometimes
called the J-source, for two reasons. (a) They may have
been J(udeans). (b) The German scholars who first
proposed this way of viewing the material wrote the
divine name as J(ahweh). There is some division of
thought about the time they may have carried out their

work. Recently many scholars have been inclined to place them during the early years of the monarchy, perhaps during the reign of Solomon (about 962–922 B.C.).

The Elohists usually refer to the deity as "God." Their collection of material is sometimes called the E-source, since (a) they may have been from the north—that is, Israelites, whose predominant tribe is E(phraim); and (b) the Hebrew word for "god" is E(lohim). There is considerable uncertainty as to the time they may have been active. There has been a recent tendency to date them at about 850 B.C.[27]

The Deuteronomists are so called because they are thought to be responsible for the collection of traditions we call Deuteronomy. In addition, it is sometimes proposed that they contributed occasional stories scattered throughout the Pentateuch. Although their material often is associated with the book discovered in the temple in Jerusalem (2 Kgs 22:8–23:25) and used as a basis for King Josiah's reform (621 B.C.), it usually is supposed that the collection began earlier, as a basis for King Hezekiah's reform efforts (2 Kgs 18:1-8). Thus we might date its compilation roughly 700–621. It often is called the D-source, for obvious reasons.

The Priestly Writers' material is called the P-source because of its concern with the duties of the Aaronite priests and the rituals to be carried out in the sanctuary. There has been considerable debate concerning its date, with 550–450 B.C. covering most positions.

---

[27]See "Elohist," *IDBS*. Some scholars believe this material was never a separate continuous collection, but the gradual addition of individual stories to J.

In order to enhance the reader's ability to recognize the four sources the documentary hypothesis proposes, some of the characteristics which scholars have isolated are listed in the chart on page 40.[28] But first, some observations are in order.

The categories are not absolutely exclusive. Thus while E tends to have the deity appear to humans in a dream or by sending an "angel" (messenger), such beings also may appear in J. Designations may shift as a collection progresses. Thus while E uses Elohim ("God") prior to the time of Moses, it may use the divine name Yahweh ("the Lord") thereafter. Certitude about the vocabulary of a given collection depends upon scholars' ability to say precisely where that collection begins and ends and which stories belong to it. While there has been a general consensus as to most of these matters, there is just enough uncertainty about some details to make absolute lists impossible.

We will now explore the growth of the collections. Several centers for the initial collection of the traditions (prior to JEDP) have been suggested. The tribe might preserve stories about its ancestors: their birth, exploits, and sayings. And thus we have, in Genesis, traditions about each of the three Patriarchs and about each of the twelve tribes of Israel (sons of Jacob). The priests at a sanctuary might be interested in preserving stories about it. When did it begin? How did it get its name? What deities have revealed themselves there? (Note Gen 28—the way the sanctuary at Bethel was founded.) What legislation was enacted there? What treaties were concluded within it? The royal house would be anxious

[28]See Otto Eissfeldt, *The Old Testament* (New York: Harper & Row, 1965), pp. 182-99.

CHARACTERISTICS OF THE FOUR COLLECTIONS

	J	E	D	P
1. usual designation for the deity	Yahweh ("the Lord") (rarely "Lord God": Gen 2–3)	Elohim ("God") until Exod 3	Yahweh your God	God; God Almighty
2. pre-Israelite inhabitants of Canaan	Canaanites	Amorites	Amorites and Canaanites	
3. where the Torah was received by Moses	Mt. Sinai	Mt. Horeb	Mt. Horeb	Mt. Sinai
4. the human attitude when the deity appears	comfortable	anxious	afraid	
5. manner by which the deity is often revealed	in human form (anthropomorphism)	in dreams; by messengers (angels)	voice is heard; no human form	voice is heard; no dreams or messengers
6. when the worship of Yahweh began	at the start of human history (but contrast Gen 4:1 and 4:26)	at the time of Moses (Exod 3:14)		at the time of Moses (Exod 6:3)
7. who may serve as a priest	members of any of the 12 tribes	members of any of the 12 tribes	Levites only	Aaronides only
8. method of referring to months of the calendar	by name	by name	by name	by number

Characteristic Expressions: D: other gods; that your days may be long; a mighty hand and an outstretched arm; the land which you are entering to take possession; which I command you this day

P: these are the generations; throughout your/their generations; be fruitful and multiply

to preserve records of its accomplishments, its genealogy, and so on. Indeed, royal archives are well attested
in the ANE. Elders might serve as preservers and
reciters of folk literature such as etiologies.

But how did these smaller collections, tribal or local,
begin to be joined into larger wholes? One factor would
have been the settlement of various groups in the land of
Canaan. Abraham's group from Mesopotamia had
settled among the Canaanites. Some of their descendants went down to Egypt, while others may have stayed
behind. Those who escaped from bondage brought with
them a "mixed multitude" of other oppressed peoples
(Exod 12:38). They were joined by other tribes,
especially the Kenites, as they wandered in the
wilderness (Judg 1:16). Cities in the land of Canaan also
united with them (Josh 9); indeed, it recently has been
proposed that large elements of the Canaanite lower
class may have revolted against the local city-state rulers
and that they all merged to form a new social reality,
"Israel."[29]

All these population elements will have contributed
their own traditions to a total "story." Those who
previously never heard of Abraham may have been
willing to accept him as their ancestor. In analogy with
our own American society, we might remember that
post-1776 immigrants celebrate the Fourth of July just as
if their ancestors had been here to participate in that
struggle. It becomes their story, too, because they
identify with the ideals of the American Revolution.

As an illustration of the possible combination of

[29]See "Government, Israelite" and "Israel, Social and Economic
Development of," *IDBS*; also Norman Gottwald, *The Tribes of
Yahweh* (Maryknoll, N.Y.: Orbis Books, 1979).

traditions, note the story in Genesis 2, which traces the human race back to a single individual, *ha-'adam,* "the human being," or "the earth-creature."[30] This might be compared with the folk tradition of tracing all Assyrians back to a "Mr. Assyria" (Gen 10:22) or all Egyptians back to a "Mr. Egypt" (Gen 10:6). Hence, all humans could be said to have descended from a hypothetical "Mr. Human Being." Then in Genesis 4:26, we encounter an individual named Enosh, also meaning (in a different Hebrew dialect) "Human Being." It is possible that two accounts of human origins have been combined, each handed down by a different constituent-part of Israel. When the groups are merged into a social totality, this is reflected genealogically: Enosh becomes the grandson of Adam.

Another possible example of such merger may be reflected in Exodus 6:3, where we are told that the Patriarchs worshiped the deity as *'El Shadday* ("the God of the Mountain(s)," often erroneously translated as "God Almighty"), since the name Yahweh (usually rendered into English as "the Lord") had not been known before the time of Moses. But in Genesis 4:26 we are told that the name was used even during the lifetime of Seth! And the Patriarchs are said to have addressed the deity by that name (e.g., Gen 15:1-2). We may conclude plausibly that within Israel, one group traditionally had worshiped Yahweh from antiquity (a J

---

[30]Note the presence of the definite article ("the"), which rules out a proper name. Indeed, contrary to many English translations, "Adam" does not occur in Gen. 2–3 (J). He makes his appearance in the later P material (Gen. 5:1). The words *'adam* ("human being") and *'adamah* ("earth" or "soil") are related—apparently derived from the verb *'adam* ("to be red in color"). See "Adam," *IDB.*

tradition), whereas another group had learned the name only at the time of Moses (an E tradition).

In sum, geographic proximity and other factors had brought about a political and social unity, and with it, the necessity for a unity of religion and tradition.

The next stages of collection were those of JEDP. Leaders of the new community (Israel) would have felt the need to answer questions about its past and future. If the Yahwist collection took shape during the Davidic-Solomonic period, Israel would have been a newly emerged international power, needing theological direction.[31] How had it come into being? Was it by accident that the people had escaped Egypt, survived in the wilderness, and settled in the land . . . or was it the manifestation of an ancient promise to the Patriarchs (Gen 12)? Should the community continue to expand its armies and boundaries and become a great military and economic power, as Solomon apparently would like it to become . . . or should it be the people of God, through whom all the people of the world will be blessed (Gen 12)? In this time of great political, architectural (building the temple and other public buildings), intellectual (the wisdom literature—psalms, songs, proverbs, etc.), and economic growth, should it not beware of the dangers of untrammeled desire for knowledge (Gen 2:15-17)? Should it not remember that, after all, we are dust and to dust we return (Gen

---

[31]The reader should be aware that there is division of thought about the date of J, as well as about its purpose. My approach is roughly that of W. Brueggemann, "Yahwist," *IDBS,* following Gerhard von Rad, *Genesis,* Old Testament Library Series (Philadelphia: Westminster Press, 1961), pp. 27-30.

3:19)? While the monarchy does appear to have God's blessing (2 Sam 7), it has limits and needs direction.

The J collectors allegedly tried to answer questions like these by gathering many of the old, familiar stories and arranging them into a "theological" history. They did not include all the stories that were available, but only those best illustrating what they thought needed to be said at that time.

But what were the changing conditions which, in scholarly opinion, necessitated subsequent stages of collection? If the Elohist collection took shape a century or so after the founding of the monarchy, and in the north (Israel)—the section that had rejected the Davidic monarchy which ruled Judah where the Yahwists had worked—we might expect slightly different emphases. We learn from the books of Kings that there was a steady erosion of the old values, and we hear in the prophets a cry for a return to those values. Not surprisingly, then, the E tradition contains stories stressing the need for faith and obedience, for renouncing idolatrous practices, and for renewing covenant vows (Gen 35:1-4; 42:21-22). In view of the increasing influence upon Israel of Canaanite religion, which featured statues of the deity, it is not surprising that E's stories downplay the tendency which one finds in J, to describe God in human form. God usually appears indirectly, in a dream (Gen 20:3) or through a messenger ("angel"—22:11; 32:1).

If the Deuteronomic collection took place in the late seventh century as the foundation document of reform efforts by the Judean kings Hezekiah and Josiah, then we would expect it to reflect the needs of that time. A major need, apparently, was to close down the various regional temples where Canaanite influence was making major inroads into the traditional Israelite faith. The prophets sometimes condemn such places by name (Amos 5:4-5; Hosea 8:5); and Josiah indeed destroyed many (2 Kgs 23:4-20). The Deuteronomists had records of an old tradition which stated that after the people occupied the land of Canaan, God would choose a place for his name to dwell (Deut 12:5, 11, 21; 14:23). Although possibly that place formerly was understood to be Shechem, fortunately for the Deuteronomists and for King Josiah, the tradition had not said so specifically! So perhaps it now could be taken to mean Jerusalem! Thus worship could be centralized in the capital city, and strenuous control could be exercised over its form (2 Kgs 23:21-23).

A related problem was that previously, there had been no regulations limiting access to the priestly office. Moses, in one tradition, had chosen young men from all the twelve tribes (Exod 24:4-5). Elijah had conducted sacrifice at Mt. Carmel, although he did not belong to a priestly family (1 Kgs 18). But the Levites had preserved or cultivated an old tradition which considered them not only to be legitimate priests, but also proposed that they alone should exercise this office (Exod 32:25-29). This tradition was now incorporated into the Deuteronomic materials and enacted as part of Josiah's reform (Deut 33:8-11). With the outlying sanctuaries shut down by Josiah, their Levitical staff would need to journey to Jerusalem and serve in shifts (cf. Luke 1:8), under the more "orthodox" central administration of the Zadokite priesthood there.

If the Priestly Collection took shape during and/or after the Exile, then the religious needs of the people would have been radically new and the previous collections (JED) inadequate to meet them. For example, how could one continue to believe in the promise to Abraham—land, endless offspring, being a blessing to others (Gen 12:1-3)—when the land had been captured by the Babylonians and many people exiled from it; when thousands of people had died from warfare and disease; when one was ridiculed by one's neighbors rather than being admired and having influence over them (Ps 137:1-3)? How could one keep one's identity—attend the temple, keep the festivals of Weeks and Booths and all the others commanded in JED (e.g., Exod 12:14; Deut 16:1-17)—when the temple had been destroyed; when one could not journey there from captivity in Babylon, even if the temple still existed? How does one refrain from accepting the values of one's captors, a tendency against which the author of Isaiah 40–55 argues (45:20; 46:1-2)? Should the people, upon their return home, reinstitute monarchy in accordance with 2 Samuel 7 or turn to some other form of government? Was it possible to use some such form as Israel had had in the wilderness, before kingship was instituted (elders, priests)?

The Aaronide priests gathered every tradition that could be found, in order to speak to such needs. The resultant material proposed that leadership by Aaronide priests should replace monarchy; major emphasis should be placed upon the sabbath and upon circumcision as reminders of identity, since those could not be taken away by exile; stress should be placed on dietary laws, since they help to set Israel's way of life apart from her neighbors; etc.[32]

[32]See "Leviticus," *IDBS,* and in *The Interpreter's One-Volume Commentary on the Bible,* ed. Charles M. Laymon (Nashville: Abingdon Press, 1971); also "Aaron, Aaronides," *IDBS.*

Since this material may have been put together over the centuries by several diverse groups of theologians . . . and since their purpose was not to be "historians" in the modern sense of the term, we need not be surprised that it has inconsistencies. For example, in Genesis 35:19, Rachel dies, but in 37:10, she apparently is still alive!

That we notice such things does not mean that we are smarter than the biblical authors or editors . . . or that they were bad historians . . . or that we have a problem of "inspiration" on our hands! The editors were concerned more with good theology than with good chronology; they wrote in order to enable Israel to realize her destiny as "a kingdom of priests" (Exod) and "a light to the nations" (Isa) rather than to be impeccable secular historians.

Problems. The sources/collections (JEDP) as I have outlined them are not nearly so coherent and unified in actual scholarly discussion as my brief, simplified presentation might suggest. No sooner did they begin to be isolated and defined than scholars began to notice tensions within them, and thus subcollections were proposed. Thus we have within J, two accounts of Esau, the first born, being replaced by Jacob in Isaac's favor (Gen 25:29-34; 27:1-40). Again, we have two J accounts of the proliferation of humankind: the descendants of Cain (Gen 4:17-24), who are said to be the ancestors of all tent dwellers, cattle raisers, musicians, and metallurgists; and the descendants of Seth (4:25-26). Note that if both accounts were written by the same author, there would be no nomads, cattle tenders, musicians, or blacksmiths among Seth's descendants! Thus as early as Rudolf Smend (1912), it was proposed that there might

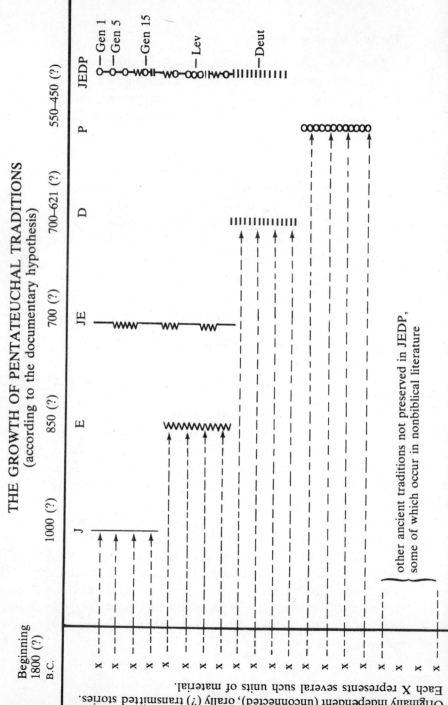

THE GROWTH OF PENTATEUCHAL TRADITIONS
(according to the documentary hypothesis)

be a J-1 and a J-2 source.[33] Similarly, various scholars have proposed multiple sources within E and P.

The variety of opinion about the number, boundaries, and purposes of the proposed subcollections does not inspire confidence that scholars are on firm ground when they talk about such matters. At the same time, such proposed subcollections tear at the fabric of the large collections. After all, it was the supposed continuity from one unit of tradition to another that led to the idea of JEDP in the first place. Now the continuity starts to break down!

Even if scholars agreed on the number of sources/collections, there always has been debate about the contents of each. To which does a particular story/chapter/verse belong? Some chapters defy confident assignment (e.g., Gen 14). Others are not "pure"—that is, a chapter may be divisible into more than one source. For example, in Genesis 50, verses 1-11, 14 usually are assigned to J, while vv 15-26 are assigned to E, and vv 12-13, to P. In some cases, the separation into possible sources takes place in mid-verse: In Genesis 2:4, concluding P's creation account are the words, "These are the generations of the heavens and the earth when they were created"; beginning J's creation account are the words, "In the day that the Lord God made the earth and the heavens." While such mid-verse division often is clearly justified (as here), at other times the reasons advanced by scholars are less convincing. Disagreements abounded, finally leading to the virtual abandonment of source

[33]See "Pentateuch," *IDB*; also see Ernst Sellin and Georg Fohrer, *Introduction to the Old Testament* (Nashville: Abingdon Press, 1968), pp. 130, 159-65; Eissfeldt, *The Old Testament*, pp. 168-69, 191-99.

criticism as a fruitful enterprise. To some, the excesses
seemed to call the entire enterprise into question. In any
case, as long as there are numerous questions about the
contents of the sources, it will hinder certitude about
their characteristics and purpose.

Particularly troublesome are spots such as Genesis
20:18, which mentions "the Lord" (usually a J
indicator), whereas elsewhere, the story refers to the
deity six times only as "God" (ordinarily an E
indicator).[34] Clearly, the basic story is E, with an
apparent J addition at the end; this is curious if J is the
earlier collection! Because of a number of such
instances, scholars have resorted to the work of a
supposed (and probably necessary) group of ancient
editors (redactors) who combined J and E (hence R[JE]).
Their purpose in Genesis 20:18 presumably was to
remind the reader that the "God" *('elohim)* about whom
they had been reading for seventeen verses, was none
other than Yahweh! This may seem plausible until we
note the date suggested for R[JE]—around 700 B.C., when
refugees from the northern kingdom fled south to Judah
at the fall of Samaria in 721, taking with them their
traditions and thus presumably necessitating a joint
edition. But would anyone, at that late date, need to be
reminded, when reading a sacred text about Abraham,
that "God" was actually Yahweh? More logical to me is
the possibility that such a clarification took place much
earlier, when diverse groups were being united to make
up Israel. Such groups would have included both *'elohim*
worshipers and Yahweh worshipers. In any case, the
necessity for such alleged redactional verses raises

[34]V. 4 is no exception—the word rendered "Lord" is not the divine
name Yahweh.

questions as to our certainty about the points at which one source ends and another begins.

Scholars have argued the relative dates of the sources, and only at the time of Wellhausen (1878), did a concensus emerge for the sequence JEDP. Some scholars still maintain the older idea that P is earlier than D. And the theory that E is earlier than J always has had its advocates. To be sure, the data are scarce, and interpretations not always compelling. While there is general consensus at present about the relative sequence—JEDP—the absolute dates have been more widely debated. The recent tendency has been to push, the dates backward from Wellhausen's suggestion (in J's case, from about 850 to about 950).

To the extent that purpose depends upon the conditions under which a document is produced, it is precarious to speak with confidence about the theology of the various sources as long as there is debate about when and where they were written. This is especially true of the J collection. Perhaps the majority opinion at present, at least among American scholars, is that J was a response to the prideful secularism of the Solomonic age. But both date and resultant theology have been questioned substantially.

What is the extent of the sources: Where do they begin, and where do they end? Debate about beginning points has all but ceased: J begins at Genesis 2:4*b*; E begins at Genesis 15:2; D is a special case, and most recent scholars doubt the older idea that there are traces of it from Genesis through Numbers; and P begins at Genesis 1:1.

It is the location of the ending of the sources that

presents the greatest problem. And if one cannot be
confident about that, then certainly the list of their
possible characteristics will be restricted and the overall
purpose will remain clouded. There have been several
proposals.

Some think that sources J and E extend from the early
chapters of Genesis through the story of the founding of
the monarchy and perhaps to the coronation of Solomon
in 1 Kings 2. That is, we would expect the story of Israel
to be recounted down to the time of the Yahwist, which
some have dated in the Solomonic era. Thus scholars
have spoken of the JE story as spanning eight books—an
Octateuch.[35]

Other authorities believe that J and E extend through
Joshua and conclude with the conquest of the land. It is
to be expected that the promise to the Patriarchs ("to
your descendants I will give this land"—Gen 12:7 and
elsewhere) would come to realization before the end of
the story. And indeed, a number of ancient "creeds"
(recitations of the sacred traditions—1 Sam 12:8; Deut
26:5-9; Josh 24:2-13) recite the story to just that extent.[36]
Thus some scholars have spoken of the JE story as
spanning six books—a Hexateuch.[37] Others, however,
have found the evidence for continuation into Joshua
not compelling and have placed Joshua in a separate
collection of literature (the Deuteronomic History).
Nonetheless, a Hexateuch is perhaps the predominant
view.

[35]See Eissfeldt, *The Old Testament,* pp. 241-48.
[36]See "Credo," *IDBS.*
[37]See "Elohist" and "Joshua, Book of," *IDBS*; also Gerhard von
Rad, *The Problem of the Hexateuch* (New York: McGraw-Hill,
1966).

Another theory maintains that J and E extend only through Deuteronomy, ending with Israel still outside the Promised Land and thus consist of five books—a Pentateuch. But this leaves the story unfulfilled, causing some scholars to propose that the original continuation, or ending, has been lost, or deliberately rejected by the priests when they added their material.[38]

Still others propose that J and E end near the conclusion of the Book of Numbers. This gives us a four-book work—a Tetrateuch—acknowledging that Deuteronomy belongs with Joshua–Kings as a separate work, but leaving the promise motif unfulfilled.

Several characteristics of a given source are shared with one or more others. For example, the deity is called "God" (*'elohim*) by both E and P; and "Yahweh," not only by J but by E, after Exodus 3 where the "name" is revealed. Thus it becomes precarious to assign a given story to one of the collections by this criterion, or by any other alone. Furthermore, we occasionally find inconsistency within an individual story (e.g., the Yahwist occasionally contains a "God" reference, as when the serpent addresses Eve in the garden—Gen 3:1*b*-5). How much variation can we allow and still preserve a meaningful characteristic which helps to identify a source? A combination of characteristics, rather than a single clue, is more compelling evidence for assigning a given story to one of the sources.

It must be added that the situation is clouded somewhat when one turns from use of the Hebrew text to various of the ancient versions. Thus in the Septuagint (Greek text) we sometimes find "God" where Hebrew

---

[38]See James Sanders, *Torah and Canon* (Philadelphia: Fortress Press, 1972), ch. 1.

manuscripts indicate "Yahweh," and vice versa. How can we be sure which one was the "original"?

In conclusion, we may observe: (a) We are on more secure ground for modern understanding of the text when we think of the larger (classical) collections—JEDP—and avoid over-speculation about subcollections; (b) This model is only what its name denotes: a hypothesis. It is a way of making sense of the data, even though there are some problems. Any other model also is problematic, so one should not assume that there is a trouble-free alternative. And conversely, since it is self-confessedly only a hypothesis, proponents should not assert it arrogantly, as if it were a fact; (c) Those who find fault with this model do not necessarily favor a return to the Mosaic-authorship alternative. More usually, modern scholars who have abandoned the documentary model suggest even more complex and unorthodox solutions to the problems of the Pentateuch. And to the most common such approach, we now turn.

C. Complex-of-Traditions Model

Rationale. Problems with the documentary-hypothesis (JEDP) model have continued to be bothersome to students of the Bible. It was thus inevitable that some other approach to the problems of the Pentateuch be formulated, even among those who found the Mosaic-authorship model a totally unacceptable alternative.

Could the themes of groups of stories (complexes)—for example, stories about what happened in Egypt—have served as the nuclei around which collections were built? Could the entire Pentateuch consist of a series of such independent collections, rather than containing four sustained narrative sources (JEDP) that run from beginning to end?

This new way of understanding the growth of the Pentateuchal materials had its beginnings in the way scholars understood the documentary hypothesis itself. Gerhard von Rad, working with the Hexateuch (Gen–Josh; see n. 36), proposed that four such thematic collections had been combined at an early state in Israel's history: patriarchal stories, accounts of bondage in Egypt, the Exodus, and the journey to the land of Canaan. And how did von Rad relate all this to the traditional documentary hypothesis? He proposed that among the literary contributions of the Yahwist to these older collections was the addition of the primeval history (Gen 1–11) and the Sinai traditions.

This approach was continued by Martin Noth, who further suggested that even the Sinai theme had been incorporated into the basic story long before the Yahwist, by what he called the "ground"/basic source, G, upon which he believed both J and E had drawn. Thus the creative role of the Yahwist (J) was further reduced.

If the traditional schools of collectors (JEDP) had created such complexes, or even joined preexisting complexes together, then why is there not more continuity from one to another? While there indeed may be similarities of style or vocabulary, the basic thematic collections seem to some scholars not to presuppose one another. For example, after all the repetitions of the promises to the Patriarchs in Genesis, one would suppose that the Exodus not only would be seen as the fulfillment of that promise, but also that this fulfillment would be proclaimed boldly. But on the contrary,

When the land is first mentioned, in the announcement of
the Exodus from Egypt, it is referred to as though the
promise tradition was completely unknown: "I will bring
you into a fine, broad land, into a land flowing with milk
and honey, to the cities of the Canaanites, Hittites,
Amorites, Perizzites, Hivites and Jebusites" (Ex. 3:8).
Not a word about the patriarchs already having lived in
this land for generations, nor about God having promised
to give this land to them and to their progeny as a lasting
possession. It is indeed a good and fruitful land but it is
also an unknown, strange land, in which many foreign
nations live.[39]

The more numerous or extensive the complexes
(building blocks) the Yahwist is assumed to have
utilized, the less room for editorial shaping of them and
thus the less clarity as to the Yahwist's theological
purpose.

Therefore Rolf Rendtorff has suggested that, rather
than beginning with the isolation of the smallest units of
tradition, as the JEDP source critics tended to do, we
concentrate upon the intermediate state of tradition-
gathering—upon complexes (themes) such as von Rad
and Noth had utilized. Furthermore, he proposes that
we do this without assuming that the usual collectors
(JEDP) had played a role in the process. Let the
necessary collectors emerge from analysis of the data,
rather than allowing them to be carried over, by force of
habit, from older approaches.

[39]Rolf Rendtorff, "The 'Yahwist' as Theologian? The Dilemma of
Pentateuchal Criticism," *Journal for the Study of the Old Testament*
3 (July 1977):9. His proposal (the complex-of-traditions model), pp.
2-10, is evaluated by a number of scholars in the same issue, pp.
11-56.

Rendtorff has isolated the following complexes: the primeval history (Gen 1–11); the patriarchal stories (divisible into Abraham, Isaac, Jacob, and Joseph complexes); the Exodus experience; events at the sacred mountain (Sinai/Horeb); wandering in the wilderness; and the settlement of the land.

Limiting his initial investigation to the patriarchal stories, he noted that the various individual episodes (narratives of events) seemed to have been joined together by means of editorially inserted speeches which convey the promise from God to the Patriarch. But such a joining together cannot have taken place all at once, since growth in the contents of the promise is perceptible. Of the various elements in the total promise (divine guidance, offspring, land, and being a blessing to others), he proposes that the earliest was a belief in divine guidance and that the other elements in Israel's understanding of the promise grew later. Even within a given element, there seems to have been a growth in the understanding of its scope. For example, the land sometimes is promised to Abraham himself (Gen 13:17); then to Abraham and his descendants (26:3; 28:4); then (latest?) to future generations only (12:7; 24:7). If we turn to the "blessing" part of the promise, it is sometimes (earliest?) Abraham himself who will affect it (12:3; 18:18); then Abraham and his descendants (28:14); then (latest?) the descendants alone (22:18; 26:4).

How can one speak of the traditional collections (JEDP), in view of such a long and complicated development? And if there were such collectors, would we not expect a given theme to carry over clearly to the other complexes? Rendtorff's conclusions: There is no

continuous, theologically consistent source running
through the Pentateuch. Rather, the complexes developed in relative isolation, each with its own theological
tendency and peculiarities of vocabulary and style.
Rendtorff is skeptical about dating the various stages of
development within a complex.

When were the various complexes combined?
Rendtorff proposes two stages: (a) a postexilic
Deuteronomic effort, which imposed, however
slightly, upon the other complexes, the idea that the
promise had been realized. The overall effort seems
related to the Deuteronomic history (Deut–Kgs), and
this results in a loosely organized work stretching from
Genesis through Kings; and (b) a priestly effort, which
contributed elements to the various complexes (genealogies, ages, dates, etc.—much that ordinarily is
associated with P in the documentary hypothesis),
although the material never existed separately as a
continuous "source."

The preexilic prophets (eighth through sixth cent.
B.C.) make few references to Pentateuchal traditions.
Would we not expect them to do so frequently, if JE by
then was in existence and widely accepted as an
authoritative version of the "sacred story"? Does this
not suggest that such formulations (the complexes) are
to be dated later—that is, are postexilic?

Problems. Materials outside Genesis *do* refer to the
promise motif (e.g., Exod 2:23-25; 6:2-9; 13:5, 11;
32:13). Rendtorff, however, thinks that these are not
integral to the growth of the complexes in which they
occur, but have been added editorially when the
complexes were combined.

The deity reveals himself, in the Egypt complex, as the God of Abraham, Isaac, and Jacob (3:6, 13, 16; 4:5). Does this not imply that the promises made to the Patriarchs now are about to be fulfilled? Rendtorff believes not. To him, the continuity inferred is in revelation, not in the content of a promise.

The Sinai complex refers back to both the patriarchal and the Egypt experiences (Exod 19:4; 32:1, 7, 11-12, 23). Rendtorff notes that the references are surprisingly few.

The wandering-in-the-wilderness complex refers back to the experience in Egypt (Exod 16:3, 6, 32; 17:3; Num 11:5, 18, 20; 14:2-4; 16:13; 20:4-5; 21:5). Rendtorff notes that the references are not to a saving event, as we might expect, but serve only as a contrast between the availability of food in Egypt and its scarcity in the desert.

The settlement-of-the-land complex contains references to the promise to the Patriarchs and to the Exodus (Num 20:15-16; 32:11; 26:4; 33:1). Rendtorff remarks that these are very few, in view of the fact that the promise at last has begun to materialize!

Materials in the patriarchal complex sometimes refer ahead to the others (Gen 15:13-16; 46:3-4; 50:24-25).

Materials in the Exodus/Egypt complex refer ahead to the conquest (Exod 13:19).

Were all the bridge passages added later (non-J), as Rendtorff tends to propose?

The opinion that the preexilic prophets do not cite Pentateuchal traditions is subjective. The question is: How explicitly do they do so?

D. From Scroll to Printed Text

Thus far, we have talked about the way the Pentateuchal materials began as isolated oral units and were gathered and edited in various states (according to which model the reader may adopt). We cannot assume that the written form of the material began with a single manuscript; it probably was committed to writing at about the same time in various places, incorporating small local variations. We know, for example, that following the Exile (587 B.C.) there were large Jewish communities in Babylonia and Egypt, as well as in Palestine. Even if those communities had taken with them identically worded traditions, local variations soon would have developed. And thus the Septuagint, a translation into Greek of the tradition as it existed in Egypt in the third century B.C. is slightly different from the Hebrew texts that have come down to us from Palestine and Babylonia. In the same manner, the Palestinian shape of the tradition (largely known from the Dead Sea Scrolls) is slightly different from the Babylonian (largely contained in the printed Hebrew Bible). And within each of these three major areas, there would be hundreds of manuscript copies of the tradition, each with minute variations.

THE BRIDGE BETWEEN PAST AND PRESENT: THE ASSUMPTIONS OF THE INTERPRETER

CHAPTER TWO

I. Interpretation Is Necessary

Books about the Bible, and trained scholars to write them, and careful reflection on the part of readers would not be necessary if the words of the biblical writers were self-evidently clear and if everyone agreed about what those writers had intended to say. On the contrary, we are aware that persons ancient and modern have argued about the possible meaning of individual passages and that denominations within the Church have formed around differences of opinion about the overall meaning of the Bible.

A. Lack of Clarity

Standing between the modern reader and the ancient writers are a number of barriers that make interpretation necessary, and in some cases, quite difficult.

A language barrier. The biblical books were written in languages that are foreign to most modern readers, and this results in losses that no translation can overcome. It often is difficult to translate even the simplest expression from one modern language to a similar one without loss of meaning. Hence the Italian proverb—A translator, a traitor. How much more difficult it is to translate complicated expressions from an ancient language, especially a non-Indo-European language such as Hebrew, to English! Let me mention a few aspects of the difficulty.

We may not know the original meaning of a word. For example, in Leviticus 11, verse 16, we are given a list of animals which Israelites were forbidden to eat. But unfortunately, the modern equivalent of some of the names cannot be determined. Is it the "desert-owl" that is forbidden (NEB), or is it the "ostrich" (RSV)? The precise meaning of the Hebrew *(bat hayya'anah)* is unclear, which might occasion consternation for those who live in an area where this creature is available for food! A comparison of various translations, and a glance at the footnotes where alternative renderings are listed, will produce hundreds of instances of such uncertainty.

Words may have an emotional overtone that is impossible to convey through mere linguistic equivalence. To use a modern illustration, the word "quisling," used as a synonym for "traitor," will not evoke or express the intensity of animosity in the United States that it might in Norway, where Vidkun Quisling, the local puppet of the Nazis, lived. Again, note that the term "redneck" has an overplus of meaning beyond the literal "red" + "neck." An English-speaking person from outside our immediate culture (say, from the 1800s or from South Africa) could not be expected to understand the intonation with which the term might be delivered or to anticipate the seething anger its application might evoke. Turning then to the Bible, we might ask, How much of its vocabulary has emotional overtones important for conveying the author's intention, but beyond our ability to recover?

Translators may have used terms that either misrepresent the original intent or may be misunderstood by the reader. As an illustration of the latter possibility, note that the word "salvation," when used in the OT (e.g., Gen 49:18 RSV), may lead some modern readers mistakenly to interpret it as saving the soul from eternal punishment.

A Manuscript-Difference Barrier. The biblical books have not come down to us through the centuries in one pure form. There are hundreds of manuscripts of the OT from the Medieval period, each with minor variations in wording. The Dead Sea Scrolls, which originated in a much earlier period, contain major variations in wording (and meaning). In addition, there are ancient versions—translations from Hebrew into Greek, Syriac, Latin, and so on—which contain yet other variant readings.

As an illustration, consider 1 Samuel 14:41, which reads either:

> Therefore Saul said unto the Lord God of Israel, Give a perfect lot [lit, *thummim*]. And Saul and Jonathan were taken: but the people escaped (KJV, following Hebrew text).

or:

> Therefore Saul said, "O Lord God of Israel, why hast thou not answered thy servant this day? If this guilt is in me or in Jonathan my son, O Lord, God of Israel, give [the lot called] Urim; but if this guilt is in thy people Israel, give [the lot called] Thummim." And Jonathan and Saul were

taken, but the people escaped (RSV, following Septuagint and other ancient versions).

One can account for the shorter form in the Hebrew
text by supposing that as the passage was copied from
the original longer form, the scribe's eye skipped from
the first instance of "Israel," to the third.[1]
Other differences in manuscripts may have resulted
from diverging scribal opinion (or error) as to the way
the consonants in a given line of text should be divided
into words. This explains why Amos 6:12 reads (in KJV
and in a footnote in RSV): "Does one plow with oxen?"
which suggests a positive answer; but RSV reads: "Does
one plow the sea with oxen?" which anticipates a
negative answer. Again, depending upon which vowels
are added to the ancient unvowelled text, disagreements
may result. This accounts in part for the difference
between "In the beginning . . ." (Gen 1:1 in KJV and
RSV), suggesting an absolute beginning—creation out
of nothing—and "When God began to create . . . he
said, 'Let there be light'" (RSV footnote, cf NEB),
suggesting that the first act was to bring order from a
preexisting chaos.

Larger variations will include differences in the
number of chapters in a book (there are 151 psalms in
the Dead Sea Scroll edition of the book of Psalms, rather
than 150), and the fact that the order of chapters within a
book may be rearranged (e.g., Jer 26 in the Hebrew
Bible is the same as 33 in the Greek Bible).

These and other types of variations will become

---

[1]This was a common scribal error and has been given the name
homoeoteleuton (similar ending [of phrases]). See "Textual Criticism,
OT," *IDBS*.

evident when English translations of the Bible are compared, and attention often will be called to them in footnotes. In most cases they will have involved an interpretative value-judgment by the translator. We thus cannot say, "I will take the Bible just as it is," since "just as it is" may vary, not only from one English translation to the next, but from one ancient manuscript to the next.

An Information-Gap Barrier. The biblical writers do not always give the background information necessary for our full comprehension of their message. They may not identify themselves (Who wrote Ruth?), or tell us when they wrote (When was Job composed?), or give information about the historical, cultural, sociological, economic, and political events which shaped their message. Thus, no thanks to Isaiah himself, we must study to realize that the unnamed "invader" who will attack Jerusalem, destroying it as completely as a tree that is cut down, is Sennacherib, King of Assyria (10:27-34). Without such research, we might have assumed (as sometimes has been done) that the "shoot" that "shall grow from the stock of Jesse" (11:1 NEB) refers directly to Jesus of Nazareth, rather than to a Judean prince, just after the invasion in 701 B.C.

That the writers often do not give us such helpful information indicates, I assume, that the message was not intended to apply to all times and all places, but to a specific audience in the writers' own time. Such an immediate audience would have known the necessary background information—there would be no need to supply it. Whatever value the text has for us, therefore, is indirect and often discoverable only after detailed study.

A Cultural Barrier. When we read the Bible, we suddenly find ourselves in an environment with values and world-view often radically different from our own. For example, how can we wear blue threads in fringes on our garments (as Num 15:37-38 commanded Israel to do), when fringes are not in style these days? How can we attribute illness to demons and hope to exorcise them (as Jesus was perceived to do), when we now know about germs, which were unknown to people in the biblical world? Should we equate germs with demons and penicillin with exorcism? How can we think of God as "up there" in a heaven with "windows" through which rain comes down (Gen 7:11), when we now know that evaporation and condensation are the actual causes of rainfall, and when even the term "up" is relative? (For persons at the North and South Poles, it is in opposite directions.) How can one continue to make sense of and be obedient to the Bible, in such a radically different world?[2]

B. *Differences of Opinion*

Interpretation of the Bible would not be necessary, assuming that we knew the original meanings, if it could be applied to the present "just as it is." That this is not the case is attested also by modern differences in the way the Bible is applied. For example, what constitutes "breaking the sabbath"?

Some parts of the Bible are definite and seem to be sound advice at all times and in all places: "Those who dig a pit may fall into it" (Prov). But other parts are directed only to specific groups: "Oracle against Moab"

[2]See James Barr, *The Bible in the Modern World* (New York: Harper & Row, 1973).

(Jer); "Hear, O Israel" (Deut). How do these apply, if at all, to persons outside those groups? Still other passages—indeed, the vast majority—are directed toward Israel in specific circumstances which will not be repeated. For example, Ahaz is advised by the prophet Isaiah (ch 7) to believe and have faith that God would deliver Judah from the Syro-Ephraimitic alliance (about 735 B.C.). We cannot mechanically say to any group, or even to Israel generally or to the Church, "Just believe in the Lord; he'll take care of it!" since that is not what Isaiah said. We modern readers are not Ahaz, and we are not threatened by that ancient alliance. To be sure, some of us may conclude that we can expand his meaning to include our own situation, but that is, of necessity, an interpretation.

In conclusion: Whether they be scholars, pastors, or lay people, all readers of the Bible are interpreting it, even though they are not consciously aware of being interpreters.

II. The Nature of the Interpreter

A. Impulsive Decisions

We may assume too quickly that we know what the text means. This may happen, strange as it sounds, because we have been overexposed to the Bible; because we are too familiar with it. We live in a (supposedly) Christian country, where even politicians quote the Bible as a means of gathering support; some radio and television stations beam their interpretation of it on a full-time basis; pastors talk about it with great enthusiasm; we may read selections from it in a daily devotional guide; and we may even be able to recite verses, learned as a meaningless string of words at our mother's knee. The Bible may thus be so familiar that we feel we do not need to study it seriously. We know, almost by instinct, what it should say. After all, have we not been told that Christianity and the "American way of life" are so intertwined as to be the same thing? All one need do, then, is breathe the local air, and one will acquire a doctoral degree in biblical studies!

One might compare this state of affairs with many people's knowledge of the United States Constitution. We have a general acquaintance with our "rights" and "freedoms," and yet not many of us could quote the Constitution beyond the first sentence. As a consequence, we sometimes are shocked to find that the Supreme Court justices, who are experts in the field, interpret the Constitution in ways that run contrary to our feelings about what it ought to say! A few years ago a group of persons reworded the Bill of Rights and then asked people on the streets if they would sign their names to the untitled document. Almost 60 percent refused to sign it, and some actually denounced the ideas as dangerous to the American way of life!

There is a sense, therefore, in which only a general familiarity breeds lack of understanding. We may not study a document in detail because we think there is no need for us to do so. In just this fashion, we may be overly confident if we have only a superficial knowledge of the Bible. Many readers might be inclined to skim rapidly through Genesis 1, saying to themselves, "It tells how long it took God to create the world—everybody knows that!" or "It's interesting to compare this approach with Charles Darwin's theory of evolution." And thus we are so familiar with popular, superficial interpretations, so convinced of what it "ought to say," that we may not notice that the story continues beyond chapter 1, through 2:4. Is the conclusion of the story, which informs us that God rested at the completion of creation, relevant to the "point" of the chapter? Has that point anything to do with the timetable of creation? Apparently not! (We will return to discussion of this passage.)

B. *Personal Needs and Preconceived Opinions*

The Bible not only *must* be interpreted in view of its nature, but it also *will* be interpreted, consciously or unconsciously, through the nature of the reader. That is, it is impossible for us to read the Bible (or any literary work, for that matter) with a "blank" mind and thus assume that it will have a direct and unimpeded opportunity to communicate precisely what the author wanted to say. Rather, "what was said" must filter through a human mind—a mind laden with a lifetime's accumulation of information, misinformation, value judgments, opinions about what the Bible is and says, and the concerns of the moment. Our preconceived opinions (prior understandings, assumptions about the world and the way it operates) thus function as eyeglasses through which the text must be viewed.

In one way, such "glasses" make a positive contribution.[3] A blank mind knows nothing, and thus communication with it would be impossible. It is the knowledge we share in common with the world of the biblical writers that makes it possible for them to speak to us.[4]

[3]See E. D. Hirsch, Jr., *Validity in Interpretation* (New Haven, Conn.: Yale University Press, 1967), Appendix II, E.

[4]See Gerald Downing, "Meanings," *What About the New Testament?* ed. Morna Hooker and Colin Hickling (London: SCM Press, 1975), pp. 128-29.

Thus, if Genesis 4:8 reports an unprecedented event in
human history (Cain killed his brother), it is only my
prior knowledge of murder that makes it possible for
me to comprehend the process that is being described.
Similarly, if I read that the prophet Elisha caused an
iron ax-head to float in water (2 Kgs 6:1-7), it is only my
prior knowledge—the specific gravity of iron is greater
than water—that enables me to understand that the
author intends to relate something extraordinary.
Whether I will believe that iron actually floated will
depend upon yet other prior understandings: What is
the nature of a prophetic miracle-story? Is it a reliable
historical source, or was it intended to have some other
basic purpose?[5] Again, if the text relates the activities
of a character called "God," I will be utterly baffled
unless, from my own experience, I know something of
the way gods are thought to act and to differ from
human beings. Again, if an ancient creed affirms that
God is merciful and forgiving (Exod 34:6-7), I cannot
share its full import unless I have been, at one time, in
need of that mercy.

On the other hand, our inevitable glasses may have a
negative effect. They may enable us to see, but if
improperly prescribed or not kept clean (through
disciplined study), they may distort the image. If the
lenses are made of colored (denominational) glass, the
true color of the object viewed will be slightly disguised.
And whereas our physical glasses can be removed and
their effect for good or ill immediately discovered, we
may be largely unconscious of the presence of our
mental (religious) glasses. We may assume that our

[5]See "Miracle," *IDB.*

beliefs and values, learned from parents and reinforced by community, schools, and churches, are those that any right-thinking person would believe and thus that they inevitably are the same as those of the biblical writers. We therefore may "see" things in the text that are not actually there, or be unable to see things that are intended, because we have been conditioned, or need, to understand the text in a given way. Did not Christians in the South during the Civil War, for example, tend to see in the biblical texts more support for slavery than did readers in the North? If so, was that solely because the text is ambiguous on this matter, or could it have been also that each group tended to read the text through its own cultural and economic "glasses"? Do we always hear what the Bible itself has to say, or do we sometimes hear only our own voice, cast back at us like an echo?

There are several types of needs or preconceived notions that may be brought to the biblical text by the reader.[6]

Psychological Needs. There are readers who may feel uncomfortable with an interpretation of the Bible which acknowledges that there are differences of opinion within it, or that its view of the way the natural world operates is outdated, or that there are passages whose very meaning is quite uncertain. Such readers desire more security, more certainty, than this understanding of the Bible allows and may prefer to associate with those who affirm that the Bible is infallible in all matters—medicine, astronomy, and history, as well as theology. Thus some groups within the Church will argue that one cannot admit that the Bible contains a single error in any field of knowledge, because to do so

[6]See John Newport, *Why Christians Fight Over the Bible* (Nashville: Thomas Nelson, 1974).

would be to risk doubt about its inspiration as a whole. Similarly, studies allegedly have shown that persons disillusioned by their experience in the drug culture, who subsequently become students of the Bible, tend to prefer groups that feature a dogmatic theology and a literal interpretation.

On the other hand, readers who have grown up in an overly authoritarian home or church may tend to overreact to that type of approach to life. Any rigid, dogmatic interpretation of the Bible will be rejected out of hand, because of their past history and present needs.

I have known seminary students whose personal preference for universal salvation—their inability to believe in an ultimate judgment—has led them to strive mightily to read that idea into the Bible at every opportunity and even to say that Gospel texts reflecting the idea of eternal punishment cannot be the genuine words of Jesus. Personal preference, then, can become a key to the way the Bible is interpreted.

Practical Needs. Medieval monarchs, zealous to preserve the doctrine of the divine right of kings, discouraged discussion of occasional antimonarchical tendencies in the Bible. For example, marginal notes in the Geneva Bible remarked upon the appropriateness of the midwives' action in disobeying the pharaoh's order to kill the newborn Hebrew infants. This displeased the English monarchy, since any theological justification for civil disobedience was a threat to the throne. In the United States, military "hawks" and "doves" sometimes will quote the Bible to support their opposing points of view. Indeed, a Senatorial aide recently wrote me for a supply of "snappy biblical retorts" to hurl at his employer's Bible-quoting opponents.

Generalizations About Human Nature. Based upon
our limited, culturally conditioned experience, we may
assume that the way people act in our lifetime is the way
they always have acted. Thus James Bennett, writing in
England during the Victorian era, rejected the idea that
The Song of Solomon could be a description of love
between human beings. The actions of the woman, he
proposes, are so bold as to be a violation of woman's
nature (i.e., she asks to be kissed; seeks her lover
outside the home; etc.).[7] Any modern reader will, in
retrospect, see the error that Bennett has made.

Generalizations About Social Custom. Based upon
our culturally conditioned experience, we may assume
that customs always have been the same, at least among
those who belong to the Church or to ancient Israel. For
example, Clement (first cent. A.D.) notes that in Genesis
9:20, Noah, having landed the ark, planted a vineyard,
made some wine, and got absolutely smashed. Clement
finds that statement hard to believe. Indeed, he
proposes that it must be a lie.

What would have led Clement to such an opinion? I
suppose that he must have reasoned: "I don't drink
wine; good Christians, in my opinion, don't drink it; and
Noah was like a good Christian; so it didn't happen!"
And thus Clement has remade Noah in his own image.

As a modern example of the way "glasses" have
influenced the interpreter's view of the text, consider the
statements of a popular evangelist a few years ago.
During a TV address, he told us that you can find evidence
of the Trinity in the very first verse of the Bible: "In the

---

[7]Cited in Marvin Pope, *Song of Songs,* The Anchor Bible, 7C
(Garden City, N.J.: Doubleday & Co., 1977), p. 135, from Bennett's
writings in the *Congregational Magazine* (1837/38).

beginning, God created the heavens and the earth." The
evidence, he said, is in the way the word "God" is written
in Hebrew. And then he pointed out, quite correctly, that
the word *'elohim* is grammatically plural. That is, one
would write the word "gods" in that way. So, he
reasoned, who are these "gods" who created heaven and
earth? The biblical writer must have had the Trinity in
mind, although it is not expressed explicitly!

Unfortunately, what the evangelist seems not to have
known is that plurals, in the Hebrew language, can be
used to express a singular idea, just as conversely in
English, a singular, such as "sheep," can mean one
sheep, or a flock. Furthermore, the biblical writer would
not use the singular form, even to refer to the sole God
of existence, because the singular *('el)* is the name of a
Canaanite deity! So the word in Genesis 1:1, or
anywhere else in the OT for that matter, has nothing to
do with the Trinity. But it is easy for Christians to "read"
the idea back into the OT.

C. Identification with the Wrong Actors

It is quite easy to convince ourselves that we are like
the heroes of the Bible story and quite unlike its weaker
characters. We might say, "Had I been there when
Jeremiah was tried for treason (ch 26), I certainly would
have sided with him—not with the majority who wanted
him executed!" Or, "Had I been there, I certainly would
have stayed with Jesus during his arrest and trial and not
have fled for my life, like his disciples!" Read in this
fashion, the Bible often calls others into question, but
never challenges us.

It is helpful to recall the story of the parishioner who
always congratulated the pastor for taking a strong stand

against sin. The standard remark, as he shook hands with the pastor at the door, was, "That's telling them, Preacher!" Never once did he give any indication that the message might have applied to him. Finally, there came a snowy Sunday morning when this gentleman, who lived nearby, was the only person able to attend the worship service. "Now," thought the pastor, "I wonder what his remark will be!" True to form, the response was, "That's really telling them, Pastor! Too bad they weren't here to hear it."

Here is a good rule: When we read the Bible and feel confirmed in our stance; when we hear it as condemnation of "them" . . . then be careful! There is a possibility that we have misread it and that we do not see ourselves honestly as we are. But when we read it and feel challenged; when we feel condemned, then there is a real possibility that we have read it properly and that we see ourselves as we truly are. Only those who know the reality of their own failings, their unworthiness, truly can hear and appreciate the gospel that the text proclaims.

III. Assumptions About the Bible

A. Bible Study Is a Worthwhile Activity

Whether or not we belong to the Believing Communities (the Synagogue and the Church) where the Bible is read as Scripture, it may be read for the same profitable reasons that any other classical document is read.[8]

We may read it with an interest in the past. We may admire its quality as literature (narrative style, poetic

[8]See "Literature, the Bible as," "Poetry, Hebrew," and "Wordplay in the Old Testament," *IDBS*; Samuel Sandmel, *The Enjoyment of Scripture* (New York: Oxford University Press, 1972).

constructions, irony, etc.). We may study it because of the excellence of the language into which it has been translated (e.g., KJV), or in order to better understand its great influence upon English idiom or the almost limitless allusions to it in literature and art. Scholars from a variety of disciplines might have an antiquarian interest in data it contains—on the history of Syro-Palestine, the sociology of premonarchical Israel, the Judean religious responses to exile in Babylonia.

Or we may read it because of an interest in the present. Modern secular persons may admire the often-innovative socioeconomic ideals of ancient Israel and thus be moved to support various programs in the present; they may be informed also by the Bible's realistic assessment of the human condition.[9]

For aesthetic reasons, or because of its contributions to Western culture, or because it contains perceptive questions and observations which transcend their initial time and situation, the Bible may be read beneficially.[10] And all this can be done without raising the question of its status as Scripture.

B. The Text Is Scripture

While members of the Believing Communities may read the Bible for any of the reasons mentioned, they also must read it as Scripture. That is, the text is to be read as a normative body of tradition for determining

[9]For socioeconomic ideals, see "Israel, Social and Economic Development of," *IDBS*; also Gottwald, *The Tribes of Yahweh*. For human condition, see D. Bonhoeffer, *Creation and Fall* (New York: Macmillan & Co., 1959); also "Genesis," *IDBS*.

[10]Wolfhart Pannenberg, "Hermeneutics and Universal History," *Journal for Theology and Church*, 4(1967):126-27; James Barr, *The Bible in the Modern World*, ch. 4.

the community's origins, defining its goals and hopes, judging and reforming its courses of action, and nurturing it in moments of crisis. To call a group of texts "Scripture" is not so much to make an objectively verifiable claim about the role of deity in its formulation (e.g., whether or how it is "inspired") as to accept it as foundational and essential to the community's ongoing life. On the one hand, the community is the agency that has preserved the Scripture—gathered and arranged the texts, handed them down from one generation to the next, and deliberately accepted them as authority. On the other hand, the Scriptures have preserved the community—given it identity, direction, and hope in times of tranquility, as well as support in moments of trial. Thus, the terms "Scripture" and "Church" presuppose each other: To belong to the community is, by definition, to acknowledge its Book as authoritative; and the use of the term "Scripture" is meaningless in the absence of a community which so defines it. The terms "Scripture" and "Church" thus are dialectically related.[11]

Those who belong to the Believing Communities may and do disagree as to the way this norm is weighed in relation to others: experience, reason, and tradition (e.g., the authority of Talmud in the Synagogue; the teaching of the Fathers in the Greek Orthodox and Roman Catholic factions of the Church; and the opinions of the Reformers among Protestants). That complicated and divisive problem need not detain us here, however.

By calling the texts "Scripture," we suggest many implications for their interpretation and use.

[11]David H. Kelsey, *The Uses of Scripture in Recent Theology* (Philadelphia: Fortress Press, 1975), pp. 89-97.

The texts were addressed to and accepted by a specific audience—an Israel who understood itself to have been elected by the deity for specific responsibilities. They are not basically timeless generalizations, hurled into the void. They were not intended to answer questions for those outside the community—questions such as, "How do we know that there is a God?" The community and its texts presupposed God's existence: It was a precondition of membership. Similarly, the text's guidelines for ethical behavior were intended as suggested responses for those who accepted the more-basic story of God's initiatives: They were not intended as a legal code to be imposed upon those outside the community, however beneficial we might assume that would have been. The Bible is the *community's* Book, not an imperialistic civil code.[12]

The community is not free to ignore capriciously the canonical (scriptural) norms, even if they appear on the surface to be irrelevant to modern life, or to be too difficult to follow, or too contrary to our personal dispositions. To accept the text as Scripture is to make a commitment to wrestle earnestly with it, to be open to obedience to it. While the community must interpret the meaning of the text for our present time, the text also must interpret the community (question its motives, judge its actions, pose an alternative value-system, etc.). Individual interpreters must be open to the possibility, therefore, that those perspectives they least

[12]See Fred Craddock, *Overhearing the Gospel* (Nashville: Abingdon, 1978), pp. 66ff.; Norman Gottwald, *All the Kingdoms of the Earth* (New York: Harper & Row, 1964). It must be stated, however, that the texts often mention the nations surrounding Israel, that the prophets sometimes announce oracles of judgment against them, and that hopes concerning their inclusion within the community are sometimes expressed.

want to hear may be those they are most in need of hearing. Those passages that appear to be least "relevant" may be those of which we are in greatest need. It is not merely that we are the interpreters, but we also must be interpreted by the text.[13]

Since the text basically is about the community, and since it was accepted by the community as its normative story, interpretation must be done by the community. That is, individuals within the community are not free to interpret in isolation from the group and to assume that one person's interpretation intrinsically is as good as another's. Thus pastors need to collaborate as sermons are prepared, and lay persons should discuss their understanding of the Bible. The wisdom of the group serves as a check against aberrant subjectivism. One speaks here of normal procedure, rather than of an infallible rule, since the community can and has erred in matters of interpretation and individuals may and have used the text as a means of correction. One can think, for example, of the prophets who, although they may have belonged to a small community, challenged the larger consensus concerning Israel's identity.

Furthermore, interpretation must be done *for* the community. The text is concerned primarily with Israel, a Believing Community, and not with individuals wherever they may find themselves. It is obvious, of course, that the community is made up of individuals who must act in concert if the group is to survive, and

[13]Richard C. White, "Preaching the New Hermeneutic," *Lexington Theological Quarterly* 9(1974):61-71, contrasts our treatment of biblical texts as objects to be used ("How are you going to handle that text?"), with that of art as subjects which affect us ("How does that [painting] grab you?").

that individuals do need guidance with specific problems. But the question is, Who are we? more than, Who
am I? This larger target often is ignored when the text is
read nightly for individual "spiritual enrichment."

*The goal of biblical studies done within the community
is not basically descriptive ("what the text meant"), but
interpretative ("what the text means today").* One
approaches the text not with detached neutrality, but in
accordance with its own purposes—to give life and
direction to the community that has accepted it as
essential and normative.[14]

C. Is the Text an Account of "What Happened"?

The mere statement of "the facts" was not the primary
motivation for the initial telling or the ultimate preservation of any particular story. Thus the oft-repeated
questions about a biblical story, "Did it really happen? Is
it historically true?" are irrelevant from the point of view
of the ancient narrators and collectors. To be sure,
modern readers, secular or religious, may ask those
questions, but they should not assume that a story's status
as Scripture demands a yes answer. The Synagogue and
Church read the text basically for theological purposes—it
contains the gospel which defines and sustains the
community. And thus the councils of the Church have
defined the Bible not so much in terms of its historical or
scientific correctness, or even in terms of its infallibility,
but in terms of its life-giving power. The Articles of
Religion of The United Methodist Church (derived from

[14]George Landes, "What Is the Exegetical Task in a Theological
Context?" *Union Seminary Quarterly Review* 26(1971):273-98;
Walter Wink, *The Bible in Human Transformation* (Philadelphia:
Fortress Press, 1973); Montague, *Catholic Biblical Quarterly*,
41(1979):1ff.

the Anglican church) state: "The Holy Scriptures contain all things necessary to salvation" (Art 5). That is the basic definition of the Scriptures for this denomination within the Believing Community.

Therefore, whatever the historical basis of a story may be, it is precarious to press that claim as necessary for spiritual life in the present. Thus one might avoid such arguments as: "A great fish *did* swallow Jonah! It says so right here in the text (1:17). It is a matter of faith . . . and therefore mine is better than yours if I believe it and you don't!"

Rather than asserting historical accuracy, one might begin by asking, Were the stories gathered by a religious community, or by a guild of secular historians? Do they serve a theological, or a historical purpose? Why was this story preserved, and not others? Why was it remembered in just this way? What was at stake for survival, for identity, when this story was told?

D. Critical Study Is Essential

Critical study always should play a major part in determining the meaning of the text for those who first spoke and heard it.[15] Yet one need not have formal training in order to profit from the great strides that have taken place in recent decades to unlock the meaning of biblical texts.

While it is true that many texts are almost self-evident, others yield their meaning only after detailed study, and some not even then. Thus, contrary to opinion ancient and modern, there are dimensions of the text which neither moral perfection, or conversion to the true faith, or the activity of the Holy Spirit is sufficient to

[15]See "Exegesis," *IDBS*.

illuminate.[16] Quick devotional reading, followed by a subjective "How does this strike me?" is no substitute for careful study which uses the best aids available. Merely to read the text and to pray that "God will make the meaning clear" is presumptuous, if not lazy.

Nonetheless, if the text is to be studied as Scripture, then one must go beyond the results of critical study of what the text "meant" in the past, to search for what it may "mean" now. One seeks now to embody the text—to obey it—and that takes one beyond the goals of critical scholarship. If the text speaks of "sin," scholarly study may give me some comprehension of the author's meaning, but it cannot convince me that it is a valid description of any human behavior, including my own. Least of all can such study impel me toward the alleviation of my sinful state. It is at this stage of deliberation that one's religious experience, or prayer, or the power of God (the presence of the Holy Spirit) must make a contribution to the "understanding" of the text.

E. Multiple Points of View in the Text

When I was growing up, I assumed that the Bible, from beginning to end, had been dictated by a single divine mind. It was thus harmonious at all points. If this appeared not to be the case, then the fault lay in the human understanding: If we could delve deeply enough, then all the apparent discrepancies would disappear.

Such an approach to the Bible constitutes another

---

[16]For the traditional claim that such attributes are essential, see Claude Peifer, "The Experience of Sin, Salvation, and the Spirit as Prerequisites for the Understanding of the Scriptures," *Sin, Salvation, and the Spirit,* ed. Daniel Durken (Collegeville, Md.: Liturgical Press, 1979), ch. 1.

case of looking at the text through "glasses." It is a comforting position, since it removes any uncertainties that diversity of opinion might cause. There is something at stake psychologically, therefore, in coming to the text with such a presupposition. We must be clear, in any case, that lack of diverse opinion is not a claim the Bible makes for itself. The proposal that there might be several points of view within it is not an "unbiblical" claim.

As I grew older minor discrepancies within the text began to become obvious. Where did Moses receive the Ten Commandments? Was it on Mt. Sinai or was it at Mt. Horeb? Other tensions are more serious than geographical discrepancies, however.

Does God punish one generation for the sins of another? Some events seem to suggest this, but at other times such needed "punishment" did not take place. Thus Deuteronomy (5:9) reflects one point of view ("visiting the sins of the fathers"), and Jeremiah (31:29-30) and Ezekiel (18:1-4) the other ("Each person suffers for his own sins").

What about an expectation that the dead will be resurrected? The OT has no such idea, while the NT does.[17]

What is the importance of sexuality in human life? St. Paul certainly seems less tolerant than does the author of The Song of Solomon! Paul expects the end of the world so soon that surely there would be no purpose in marriage. But the author of The Song of Solomon gives no indication that he is married to the young lady whom he so lyrically and graphically describes. Nor can we

[17]Excluding the very late passage in OT, Dan. 12:1-3 and possibly Isa. 25:6-8.

escape the song's frankness by saying that it is an
allegory of the love between Christ and the Church, for
that results from Christian "glasses" through which the
text is viewed.

Such diversity of opinion is hardly surprising, given
these facts. (a) The OT has grown over a period of at
least one thousand years, and perhaps as many as two
thousand. As times changed—as God was perceived as
working in new ways in history—it was necessary for
Israel's theology to adjust accordingly. (b) While some
issues, at a given moment in Israel's history may have
seemed clear-cut, others were more complicated.
"Truth," like reality, may be ambiguous.[18] A possible
example might be the debate regarding the institution of
monarchy (2 Sam 8–11)—is it a good thing, a channel of
divine blessing sanctioned by God . . . or is it a human
desire for security, which will lead to the undermining of
old values?

If it may be granted that a plurality of positions on
some matters may be found in the canon, then the
question may be raised as to their relative "authority" in
the present. In general, there have been two major
approaches to a solution of this dilemma.

According to one position, later is better. "Progressive
revelation" maintains that, as time progressed, either
God was revealed more fully, or Israel understood God
more clearly.

Several problems with such an approach may be
mentioned. (a) There is a danger that it could lead
Christians to a self-serving pride and to a polemic

[18]See "Hermeneutics," *IDBS*.

against biblical Judaism. (b) If rigorously pursued, it would establish Daniel and Esther as the "fullest" revelations in the OT (since they probably are latest), and 2 Peter, as the most authoritative in the NT . . . which certainly is pushing this perspective farther than many of its advocates would sanction. (c) It ties "truth" to a chronological timetable, which would sanction the claims of Islam that it is a fuller revelation than the Christian Bible.

According to the other position, early is better. This is a modern scholarly position, more than a traditional one. It attempts to discover the earliest sources by removing later layers of interpretation within a book, or smaller glosses within a paragraph. Thus one could hope to discover the exact words of Jesus behind the reports of the Evangelists, or free Amos from the distortion created when the so-called happy ending (9:8b-11) was later attached to his "genuine" message.

In addition to these more formal attempts to evaluate a plurality of stances within the biblical text, a more subjective one could be mentioned: Choose the one that appeals to you! As a matter of fact, that is quite often what we do. We have a tendency to study or to preach from a few favorite books because they arc more comforting (or we feel more comfortable when we read them) or because they support our personal or denominational doctrinal and ethical stances. Frustration in a modern society from which we feel alienated may lead us to prefer what appear to be otherworldly speculations in Daniel and Revelation, rather than the this-worldly concrete socioeconomic demands of Leviticus. One thus arranges the Scriptures in a subjective hierarchy of value—that is, value = valuable to me.

My suggestion is not a solution to resolve the tensions, but a call to appreciate their value. Diversity within the Bible is not necessarily a totally negative state of affairs to be resolved by subjective preference. Perhaps listening is more important than evaluation. Perhaps our need to be judged by the Scriptures is more important than the need to judge them. Perhaps we should take all the Canon seriously, rather than evaluating it in terms of our fixed beliefs.

It is helpful to remember that the Bible was not formed by majority vote, with the possibility that a year later, with another delegation, the contents might have been different. On the contrary, each story, each book, presupposes a Believing Community which treasured the story, found its identity affirmed in it, found itself judged by it; and hence the community repeated the story and handed it down. The Scriptures thus evolved by communal wisdom. Each unit has played perhaps a crucial role in the survival of our community. Should we therefore not listen to each, rather than presuppose that it is inferior to other units?

Will stories the community found of value in *one* age agree with the wisdom of the next? If not, does that mean that some of them are "wrong"? Dare we use the word "wrong" when we refer to Scripture? In any case, could we pronounce the wisdom of *one* generation as forever wrong, with all the situations of the future yet unknown?

Consider the case of the book of Nahum, much maligned for its vindictiveness against the Assyrians. The prophet sees God at work in the wholesale slaughter of the population . . . *surely* not a point of view Christians could endorse? Certainly this is not the God of the One who said, "Let the little children come to me?" But is it not possible for evil to be so entrenched, so bestial, that one can rejoice at its total eradication? The atrocities by Assyria seem too far away for us to comprehend. But what about the evils of slavery in our own country in more recent days? Can we not sense the power of the *Battle Hymn of the Republic* as they marched off to war? "Mine eyes have seen the glory of the coming of the Lord; He is trampling out the vintage where the grapes of wrath are stored." And in more recent days, what about the Nazis? As one stands at the national memorial in Israel, views exhibits from the death camps, reads that endless list of victims' names, sees soap made of human fat, can one not praise God for the destruction of the Nazis? Can we not hear in Nahum a word, *the* Word, which must not be extinguished?

F. The Bible "Speaks in the Language of Human Beings"

As Rabbi Ishma'el stated in the second century A.D., the Bible is not to be viewed as the very words of God, but as an inspiring or "inspired" message expressed in human terms. It is commonly said that the Bible does not contain God's words, but his Word. It is not a verbatim report of God's conversations with the authors of Scripture, such that had we been there with a tape recorder, we could have captured them exactly as they have been handed down to us. The biblical writers rather sought to express feelings, interpretations, religious experiences, and values in the language of their own time.

For example, if Moses or anyone else in the biblical period is convinced that human life is valuable and that it

cannot be taken by anyone who desires to do so, then he
is free to express this "inspired value" in any way he
chooses. He can write a long legal treatise against
murder; he can tell a story, long or short, in order to
illustrate his point; or he can express it in a simple,
straightforward commandment: "You shall not murder" (NEB). The choice is up to Moses. The words are
his—they need not be inspired, even though there is an
inspired basic conviction behind them. In any case,
succeeding generations have accepted the value and the
words in which it is expressed as worth remembering and
obeying. Thus the words have become Scripture
through the acceptance of the community.

The language used to introduce an inspired conviction
may vary. Moses says, "And God spoke all these words"
(Exod 20:1); Amos says, "The Lord God showed me"
(8:1); Ezekiel says, "The hand of the Lord was upon
me" (40:1); Jeremiah says, "The Word of the Lord came
to me" (16:1); the book of Exodus says, "The messenger
of the Lord appeared to him [Moses] in a flame of fire
out of the midst of a bush" (3:2); the book of Genesis
says, "The word of the Lord came to Abraham in a
vision" (15:1). My suggestion is that all these terms are
interchangeable; that they refer to a common type of
experience or conviction. These terms are first-millen-
nium B.C. ways of saying, "I feel impelled"; "I feel
inspired to say"; "I just had an inspired thought." They
are human expressions of convictions that religious
people still have, but which we now may express in
different terms. We must look behind the individual's
language, which changes from one generation to the
next, to discover the reality it attempts to express.

Let us turn to a slightly different illustration of human

language in the Bible and the way it changes from one generation to the next. How does one explain unusual human behavior—stammering language, jerky muscular activity, radical change of personality, or entry into a trance? In the ancient world, such strange activity usually was thought to be caused by some outside force which had entered the person—it might be a god, it might be a demon, or it might be the "ghost" of a deceased ancestor. The physical and psychological realities were the same then as now, but the understanding of them and the language used to describe them has changed.

Thus the biblical writers used the vocabulary and the medical understandings of their own day. They could not do otherwise. In the OT, which does not acknowledge the existence of demons, Saul's fits of anger and mental deterioration are described as the result of "an evil spirit from God." Perhaps we should translate it as "an evil compulsion." But in the NT, a man who runs around naked, living in tombs hollowed out in the rock, is said to have "demons" (Luke 8:26-29). It would be a mistake, I think, to take that language literally, rather than to look behind it for the same reality we can observe today, but which we describe from a different point of view (the view of modern psychiatry, although much of that terminology, in the same manner, will be out-of-date in the future).

IV. The Move from Past to Present

A. Subjectivity

The application of the text to life in the present—"what it means," as opposed to "what it meant"—is a subjective

activity. While there may be generally recognized
guidelines to help us recover the ancient meanings,
there are very few widely accepted guidelines to help us
move from "then" to "now." This is the case for a
variety of reasons.

What it "means" presupposes a view of what it
"meant." Not only are there various levels of past
meaning, but some of them may not be clear. Which . . .
if any . . . can or should speak to the present?

If our view of what it "meant" is colored by our
preconceived notions (our glasses), then our view of what
it "means" today probably will be even more colored,
since it is at this point that our personal needs come into
play. If, then, we must and do choose our norms for
applying the text to the present,[19] we have an obligation to
think about them carefully and to state them as clearly as
possible. I believe that the task is not merely intuitive or
passive ("Just trust God to make the meaning clear!") and
need not be entirely subjective. Nonetheless, *any* attempt
to suggest guidelines may meet resistance as a matter of
principle. It may be denounced as a scholarly omnipo-
tence trap ("Don't try to tell *me* how to use the
Bible!")—an attempt to control the Spirit of God, which
should guide all application of Scripture. But does not
devotion to the Scriptures demand careful, consistent
reflection upon our assumptions about the way it may
address us in the present?

B. Continuity

*The application to the present should not lose sight of
the way the text is used within the Bible itself.* Narrative
should be used as narrative. Listen for a story's main

[19]Hirsch, *Validity in Interpretation,* ch. 2.

point, rather than trying to derive catchy ideas from passing details. If the Pentateuch was basically Israel's "identity-forming narrative," then we may need to hear it in the same way our spiritual ancestors did. We read of Abraham's failures, and we understand ours; we read of the ground of his hope, and we find hope in the present. The human condition under the covenant, past and present, comes into focus. To relate the Word to the present often is merely to tell the Story. To repeat the Story is to make a theological affirmation.

Avoid simplistic moralizing.[20] Unless the original point of a story was to discourage the reader from becoming like its characters, then we should not move directly to that usage, either. If a sermon concludes with a stirring exhortation—"Oh, that all of us would be like David, when he did so-and-so"—then that preference is stated on the pastor's authority, not on the authority of the Bible, unless the Bible contains the same suggestion. Furthermore, the selection of possible moral examples usually will be in accordance with the preconceived values of the selector. Whatever one's present values are, there probably is an appropriate biblical model— one not necessarily condemned in the Bible itself. Abraham may be cited as a model of faith (Gen 15:6; Rom 4:3), but we may forget that before long, he had betrayed the promise a second time (Gen 20:1-2). We must thus learn to look beyond the morality of a story's characters to the overall reason the Community preserved the story, if we can discover it. It is not so

[20]The dangers of this very common approach are outlined in Leander Keck, *The Bible in the Pulpit* (Nashville: Abingdon, 1978), pp. 100-105.

much that *Abraham* is hero or villain, as that the story is about *God* as hero: It is the deity who preserves Abraham and provides for a future. Again, it is not so much that Jacob is a trickster, as that God chose him as the father of Israel.[21]

Use legal materials as a response to the gospel story. The Commandments should be presented as guidelines for the concrete expression of gratitude for the things that God already has done, rather than as grounds for condemnation of the hearer. And one should avoid unfavorable (and unjustified) comparison with the gospel found in the NT.

C. Individualization

A text that initially was addressed to Israel as a whole should not be individualized. Seek its relevance for the community in the present, before inquiring about its meaning for the individual members. Thus if the identity and future of Israel is tied up with Abraham's actions at the near-sacrifice of Isaac (Gen 22), we should not begin by treating the story as an example of the way a modern father should or should not treat his children (see ch 4, IV).

D. Spiritualization

We should not begin by spiritualizing the text by finding some present spiritual analogy to the problem of the biblical characters. The homiletical commentary in *The Interpreter's Bible* treatment of Genesis 37, at the point where Joseph's brothers have cast him into the pit, suggests that we all are in pits of mental and spiritual

[21]See James Sanders, *God Has a Story, Too* (Philadelphia: Fortress Press, 1979).

depression and that God can deliver us from such states, just as he delivered Joseph from the pit.[22] While many readers will agree that God can do so, the fact remains that this was not what the storyteller had in mind and was not the reason this story was retold over the generations. If the homiletician wants to make such a point, let him make it on his own authority, for it is not "biblical." One could just as well have made those observations by reading from a novel or the morning newspaper. The congregation does not (or should not) gather, in my opinion, to hear the ingenuity of the preacher, but the profundity of the Bible. Saddest of all is the fact that the Bible's profound point, which does not emerge until 45:4-15, is neglected.

Again, a recent sermon began with remarks on the vertigo (spatial disorientation) experienced by helicopter pilots during the attempted rescue of hostages in Iran. Then it suggested that we also can be afflicted with spiritual vertigo. It sought to illustrate this with an episode in the Bible—Esau, who surrendered his birthright in a moment of hunger (Gen 25). The implication then drawn was: Don't be like Esau! But we must ask, Is that why this particular story was told? Is Esau condemned for spiritual vertigo? Is he condemned at all? No, the story tells why Jacob, the younger and undeserving, received the blessing, rather than the older, proper, expected son—it was through no merit of Jacob's! The text has to do with the reason one society (Israel) was the instrument of God, and not the other (Edom). The modern preacher individualized the text, spiritualized it, and drew a moral lesson when none was intended.

[22]Ed. George A. Buttrick (Nashville: Abingdon Press, 1952), vol. 1, p. 754.

E. Substitution

We should not begin by substituting one group for another unrelated group. If the text is addressed to Israel, it at least should speak to those who, in the present, in some way consider themselves a continuation of ancient Israel. If Israel is condemned for idolatry, we cannot substitute the United States, a modern secular state. May the preacher arbitrarily say, "God will judge America, just as he did Israel"? Are we modern interpreters free to erase any name in the text and substitute any other that fits our fancy? If Exodus relates that God delivered Israel from Egypt, may we anticipate his deliverance of blacks in South Africa, be they Jews, Christians, Muslims, or animists? If we do generalize the text in that way, we should be aware of the interpretive steps we have taken!

F. Humanization

We should not anthropologize the text by transforming it from a story about God to one about humans. Genesis 12 tells us of God's activity in electing Abraham—an election which Abraham betrays by leaving the Promised Land and by giving away the potential mother of Israel. Since God restores all, we should not transform the story into one in which Abraham is the hero by advising, "Be a man of faith! Obey as he did!" When Isaiah encourages the community in exile to believe that it can yet accomplish its promised destiny ("I am doing a new thing"—43:19), we should not individualize this, spiritualize it, and then anthropologize it by urging, "Today is the first day of the rest of your life! Believe! Be positive! Don't look back! *You* can do it!"

LEVELS OF MEANING IN THE TEXT

CHAPTER THREE

A passage of Scripture may have as many as ten levels of "meaning," and the modern interpreter should be aware of the level that is being considered at the moment.[1] Thus it is precarious to speak, as we commonly do, of "*the* meaning." At least the following possibilities may be mentioned.

Level I. What the Author Actually Said

This level itself is much debated, and several aspects should be discussed.

A. The Literal Meaning of the Words

The literal meaning is especially important to those who believe that the Bible is "verbally (word-for-word) inspired," and that what a text "says" is what it "means"; that the Bible is "literally" true.

[1]Vern S. Poythress, "Analyzing a Biblical Text: Some Important Linguistic Distinctions," *Scottish Journal of Theology,* 32(1979): 113-37; Gerald Downing, "Meanings," *What About the New Testament?* ed. Morna Hooker and Colin Hickling (London: SCM Press, 1975), ch. 10.

On one hand, attention to this level of meaning sometimes may keep the modern interpreter from going astray. For example, if one is bothered because the current modern scientific opinion about the age of the earth (about five billion years) differs from the literal interpretation of Genesis 1 (that creation was accomplished in but six days), then one might seek to harmonize these differences through the "day = age" theory. In this point of view, the word "day" need not indicate twenty-four hours, but may be a stage of creation not unlike the epochs of modern geologists.[2] After all, the Bible itself says that "with the Lord one day is as a thousand years" (2 Pet 3:8). But attention to the literal meaning rules out such an interpretation. One could well object as follows: "If the text says that God completed the work of creation in 6 days, it means precisely that—6 *days,* and not 6 thousand-year periods, 6 epochs, or 6 anything else! I just take my Bible 'straight'!"

On the other hand, attention to the literal meaning can raise a number of difficulties.

There are about 480 words in the OT that occur only one time *(hapax legomena),* and hence the determination of their meaning is especially difficult. Words used more often also can be hard to translate. Perhaps the best-known example is the word *selah,* which occurs several times in The Psalms (e.g., 52:3, 5; 54:3; 55:7) and whose precise meaning remains a mystery. Or, turning to something a bit more central theologically,

[2]This rather common approach is allowed in The New Scofield Reference Bible, in the note to Gen. 1:5: "day" may mean only a "creative day"—"a period of time marked off by a beginning and ending."

consider the verb form *nibr^eku,* used in God's blessing of Abraham (Gen 12:3). Does it mean that others will "be blessed" through the community which Abraham will father (NIV, TEV), or that others will pray to be blessed as his clan is blessed (NJV, NEB)? Not only does this illustrate the difficulty in stating the literal meaning of the text in some cases, but it also should caution the modern interpreter not to put too much reliance upon any one translation.

Also, a given word may have more than one "literal" meaning, depending upon the context in which it is used. In English, for example, a quick check of the dictionary will show that a significant number of words have multiple meanings. The adjective "high" can mean physically tall (a building), intense (high speed), expensive (high price), exalted (high office), advanced (high school), elated (high spirits), and soon, all extended meanings of a single concept. Or think of such nouns as "hip": part of the body, part of a rose (from Old English *heope,* "briar"), and a cheer, all unrelated in origin. Similarly in the Bible, knowing what the text literally means is not merely a matter of assigning a single meaning to a word. There may be more than one thing or idea that a word means literally. Consider the various ways in which NJV renders the single Hebrew word, *ts^edaqah* (usually translated "righteousness" in the RSV): beneficence, triumph, merit, truth, and so on.[3] Failure to realize this flexibility of language (contextual meaning), by using the same English equivalent each time a Hebrew word occurs, can lead to obscurity. Such a mistaken perception of literal meaning

[3]See Keith Crim, "The New Jewish Version," *Duke Divinity School Review* (Spring 1979):187.

led to the following translation of Jeremiah 22:23, which
few will agree is a model of clarity: "Thou dwelling in
Lebanon, building a nest in the cedars, how being
compassionated in pangs coming to thee the pain as of
her bringing forth."[4]

Words themselves cannot convey the emphasis upon
which meaning may depend. In the sentence, "I am
going to town tomorrow," the meaning changes,
depending upon which word is stressed.[5] Meaning
conveyed by tone of voice is lost when material shifts
from oral to written form. An excellent biblical example
may be found in Jonah 4:11 (the punch line of the entire
book) which reads, literally: "I shall not have pity . . ."
But it is clear from the context that a question is meant,
which totally reverses the meaning: "Shall I not have
pity . . . ?" The implied answer is, "Yes, I shall."

In addition to literal meanings, words may have
"extended" meanings. Failure to realize this by taking
the text literally may cause the reader to miss the
intended meaning entirely. Here are some illustrations:

Does God have a physical body: fingers (Exod 8:19),
nose (Exod 15:8), eyes (Amos 9:8), and heart (Gen
8:21—or are these anthropomorphisms?[6] Even if we
recognize the nonliteral intent of such passages, we may
have trouble transferring this realization to other
passages. Does the Bible intend for us to believe,
literally, that God walked in a garden, searching for a

---

[4]From a translation by Julia E. Smith (1876), as cited by Bruce
Metzger, "The Revised Standard Version," *ibid.*, p. 72.

[5]I have taken this illustration from Hirsch, *Validity in Interpretation.*

[6]Anthropomorphism = Greek *anthropos* (man, human) +
morphos (change): to describe God in human terms, for the sake of
clarity and analogy.

gardener who hid among the trees (Gen 3:8-10), or that the deity stopped by Abraham's place on the way to Sodom and ate beef for lunch (Gen 18:1-8)? If so, how would those who told these stories have reacted to other biblical materials such as, "[God said to Moses] you cannot see my face; for man shall not see me and live" (Exod 33:20)? Should we not extend our understanding of such human-analogy language (which describes God as if "he" were human) to his keeping of a record book ("the Lamb's book of life"—Rev 21:27; cf. 3:5)?[7] If so, then it becomes a concrete way to tell us, "God remembers." Shall we extend it to the messengers ("angels") sent to humans (Exod 3:2)? If so, it is only an ancient way to say that God "communicated" or "acted."

Were the ancient Israelites stone worshipers, when they addressed their God as a "rock" (Ps 18:2, 31, "And who is a rock, except our God?")? Everyone will recognize this and similar expressions (e.g., God is a "shield"—Gen 15:1) as analogies (metaphors), but we may tend to forget their existence when we argue that the Bible must be taken literally.

Does blood have the power of speech ("the voice of your brother's blood"—Gen 4:10), or does fire have a digestive system ("And fire . . . consumed [lit.—ate] the two hundred and fifty men": Num 16:35)? Everyone will agree that these are personifications: the application of human characteristics to inanimate objects. Again, this serves as a warning against saying thoughtlessly, "I believe the Bible to be literally true."

[7]This masculine pronoun is itself a good illustration. The Hebrew language has only two genders (masculine and feminine), whereas English has three (adding the neuter "it"). Thus in order to speak of God in Hebrew, one must, of necessity, assign a gender to "him."

The biblical accounts sometimes contain overstatements (exaggeration; hyperbole), in order to stress the magnitude of the event described. Hence one need not believe that the writer meant that the earth literally was "split" (1 Kgs 1:40), that Abraham's descendants really are as numerous as the stars of heaven, which we now know to number in the billions of billions (Gen 22:17), or that no one in Egypt could move "hand or foot" without Joseph's permission (Gen 41:44).

The replacement of blunt language with more polite expressions (euphemisms) is no less evident in the Bible than in contemporary speech. Just as we avoid saying that a person "died" by using such phrases as "passed away," or more traditionally, "crossed over Jordan," the Bible will say, "David slept with his fathers" (1 Kgs 2:10). But this could be taken "literally" (both in Hebrew and in English) to imply sexual activity! While almost everyone would recognize the intent of this euphemism (or idiom), will they see the same possibility for the "chariot of fire" and the "whirlwind" which took Elijah away (1 Kgs 2:11)?

There are other kinds of nonliteral constructions in the Bible, but perhaps enough has been said to alert the reader to the problem of "meaning" at this level.[8] There remains, however, the problem of knowing when a text is to be taken literally and when it is not. And there is also the human tendency to permit nonliteral interpretation when it fits our own system of thought, but to condemn it in others when it leads to an understanding that differs

[8]Jacob A. Loewen, "Non-literal Meanings," *The Bible Translator* 26(April 1975):223-24; (October 5, 1975):435-40; (April 1976):201-209, gives other categories, and some of my examples have been drawn from his first article.

from ours. Even the staunchest self-proclaimed "conservative," if pressed, will admit the necessity for nonliteral interpretation, and yet may condemn others for "taking liberties with the text."

B. The Meaning of the Words in Context

That idioms, phrases and clauses, and many sentences may differ from the literal meaning of the words they contain should be clear from the previous section. When God is called a "rock," it is not a comment upon appearance or physical composition, but rather an assertion of belief in permanence and protective power. To speak of God's "feathers" (Ps 91:4 KJV; RSV, "pinions") and "wings" is not to indicate that there is a cosmic equivalent of the Big Bird of Sesame Street, but to express confidence in divine protection. To suggest that God was married to two young ladies (Oholah and Oholibah—Ezek 23:1-4) and that they had children is not to accuse the deity of bigamy, but to symbolize divine love for Samaria and Jerusalem.

It may be argued that one's primary attention should be to the sentence and not to the words. Words basically derive their meanings from sentences, and not the reverse.[9] I must not assume that I can go to a dictionary, take each word's meaning, put them all together, and understand a sentence. Words may have more than one meaning; not all the possibilities may be given (uncommon words and slang may be omitted); and the author of the text I am reading may be using words in an

---

[9]Of course, it works both ways, and this has given rise to what is called "the hermeneutic circle": How do we know the meaning of a word? We derive it from its context in the sentence. And how do we know what the overall sentence means? We see it as a collection of individual words.

unorthodox manner. Furthermore, one cannot always trust the root meaning (etymology) or historial meaning of a term to give insight into its usage in the present.[10] It sometimes is difficult to know whether a given phrase evokes the same image in us that it was meant to evoke when originally used.

How does context shed light on the meaning of the six "days" in Genesis 1, which we discussed above? Let us begin by looking at the verses which contain the problematic word "day" (5, 8, 13, 19, 23, 31). In each case, we are told that the "day" consists of an evening and a morning . . . a description of the ordinary twenty-four hour day. Furthermore, these "evenings" and "mornings" are characterized by the light of the sun and the moon (14-19)—periods of sunlight and periods of moonlight—night and day, just as we know them. The sun and moon are to regulate agricultural seasons, "days," and years, suggesting ordinary periods of time as we measure them in the present (v 14). And in the wider perspective, six of these periods lead up to the weekly sabbath. Contextually, then, there is no reason to believe that the word "day" here means anything other than a twenty-four hour period.

But what about the supposedly related passage from 2 Peter? Here also, attention must be paid to the context. The author begins by acknowledging the existence of scoffers who point out that God has not acted to keep the promise of a coming time of justice in the world (3:3-4). But the audience should not be discouraged: God has a wider perspective than do humans, and although the accumulated days of delay may seem long

---

[10]See James Barr, *The Semantics of Biblical Language* (Oxford: Oxford University Press, 1961), ch. 6.

to us, it is not so with God: "The Lord is not slow about his promise as some count slowness" (v 9). For the deity, a thousand years are as a single day is to humans (v 8). The point, then, is that God is faithful to the promise and does not reckon time as do we. Thus we cannot say that the deity is "slow." The issue is thus entirely different than that of Genesis 1; it does not say that, on any time scale, 1 day = 1,000 years.

C. The Overall Meaning of a Literary Unit

Here one is not primarily concerned with individual words, phrases or clauses, or even sentences. One could argue that the paragraph takes precedence over the sentence, just as the sentence takes precedence over the individual words, as far as meaning is concerned. One must look beyond the sentence to the wider context, to all the sentences that were intended to be understood together and to express an idea.

Consider again the account of creation in six "days." It begins in Genesis 1:1 and concludes at 2:4a.[11] In good narrative fashion, everything moves toward the "point" at the end: God rested—the sabbath was instituted in the very beginning and even God observed it. We may gather, therefore, that human beings should also observe it (that point is not explicitly made here, but elsewhere—Exod 20:8-11). If this is indeed the major "thrust" of the account, then it is important to realize that the account has *not* been moving in the direction of

[11]It may strike the modern reader as curious that a story's beginning and end do not always accord with chapter and verse divisions. It is important to realize that such divisions are not as ancient as the text itself; they are Medieval, although there were earlier types of divisions. Ch. 1 has been made to end with God's labor in creation, but that division has cut the point of the story adrift.

some other modern concerns, such as: How long did it take God to create the world? (Are modern geology and astronomy antibiblical?) How are humans related to other creatures? (Is modern evolutionary biology antibiblical?) While those may be pressing concerns for some, they were not ancient concerns, and it is only with difficulty that we can force the Bible to deal with them. The basic problem becomes, therefore, How many explicit, intended points can a literary unit have? Does the author move toward a central conclusion upon which he wants us to concentrate, or are we free to assign ultimate significance to each word, phrase, and sentence? We have seen that words and phrases cannot always be taken "literally." Moreover, some biblical material, by form, seems to move toward a major point, as in Genesis 1:1–2:4a. This is especially evident in 2:4b-25, which reaches the "point" in verse 24, which begins "Therefore . . ."

As a longer illustration, consider the book of Jonah, whose overall point has to do with God's attitude toward those outside Israel, but whose details center around a rebellious prophet who is swallowed by a great fish, within which he lives for three days and three nights. How literally shall we accept the "fish story"? Is it a vehicle for the theological point, or is it true in every detail? Or does it matter? Whether we take it literally or not, at least one should recognize the central thrust toward which the story moves in the last verse ("Shall I not pity . . .")? Perhaps literalists and nonliteralists can "agree to disagree" about such a subordinate point as the fish episode, as long as they realize the larger reality to which the author points.

Another illustration often discussed may be found in

the first chapter of Job. The hero of the story, a righteous man, suffers because of a contest between the deity and the prosecuting attorney of the divine council (the "Satan"—1:6). A number of interesting questions may be raised, some of them theologically troubling if one focuses upon the details of the story. Are there limits to God's knowledge, since Satan is asked where he has been and whether he knows Job's merits (1:7-8)? Would the deity really allow a righteous person and his entire family to suffer or die, simply in order to make a point with one of the heavenly subordinates? How do we relate this to other portraits of the deity in the Bible which stress God's justice and love? Or should these and other questions be set aside in order to focus upon the wider perspective of the chapter? Are these not merely the literary details necessary to "set up" the problem of human suffering in relation to divine justice? Whether actual or not, they function to lead us on to the reality of the problem, which the author then proceeds to discuss (chs 3:1–42:6).

It is necessary to hear a story through to its completion in order to grasp the whole meaning. We must not stop to seek the significance of details, or to see if they are all logically consistent, or to ask if they could be historically and literally true. This is illustrated by a section of George Peele's play, *The Old Wives' Tale* (c 1560). Gammer Madge is telling a story to two young pages, Frolic and Fantastic.

> *Madge:* Once upon a time, there was a king, or a lord, or a duke, that had a fair daughter, the fairest that ever was, as white as snow and as red as blood; and

once upon a time his daughter was stolen
away; and he sent all his men to seek his
daughter; and he sent so long, that he sent
all his men out of his land.

Frolic: Who dressed his dinner, then?
Madge: Nay, either hear my tale, or kiss my tail.
Fantastic: Well said! On with your tale, gammer.[12]

Failure to pay attention to the major point of a
narrative can lead us to draw theological significance from
the text where none was intended by the author (or by the
community which collected and preserved the material);
it may reside only in the mind of the reader. Theologizing
about incidents is a very common tendency among the
clergy.

Jacques Ellul notes that Jonah, having finished his
sermon in Nineveh, went outside and sat in the shade to
await the destruction of the city. This was a mistake, says
Ellul, since it implies that the prophet's task was finished
. . . indeed, that he thought God's work to be finished!
Rather, he should have realized that God's work is
never done![13] Would that not make a marvelous
sermon? It depicts our failure and God's unending
activity in our behalf. But there is a small problem! It is
Ellul who makes this point, not the author of Jonah. It is
an inference from an inconsequential incident in the
text. Thus to preach from it is to make an issue of
something that was of no interest to the author of
Scripture. Such a sermon might make a profound point,

[12]As cited by Northrop Frye, *A Natural Perspective* (New York:
Columbia University Press, 1965), p. 13.
[13]J. Ellul, *The Judgment of Jonah* (Grand Rapids, Mich.:
Eerdmans Publishing Co., 1971), p. 79.

but let us be clear: We would be manufacturing a Word, rather than transmitting the Word.

Consider another case—that of Queen Jezebel who, preparing to meet her death with dignity, "painted her eyes, and adorned her head" (2 Kgs 9:30). The writer merely notes this in passing, and while he may condemn her for a number of things, this is not one of them. It is incidental to the text. Yet, innumerable are the sermons preached by Protestant clergy in condemnation of cosmetics, using the expression "a painted Jezzy-bell." This is to draw a conclusion the Scriptures never intended; it is to use them as a pretext for one's own prejudices.

It is well to suppose that, by and large, the biblical writers had but a single purpose in mind when they produced and preserved a unit of material. The task of the modern interpreter is to recover that one, single, central idea. One must ask of the text the question it was intended to answer. One cannot make it speak to modern concerns that are alien to its intent. Thus one should refrain from selecting a single word, or phrase, or even an entire verse for sermonic treatment until one is convinced, by careful study, that such a part reflects the "point" toward which the larger unit is moving.

Level II. What the Author Meant to Say

When we are questioned about our meaning at a given point in a conversation, we may say, "I know that I *said* so-and-so, but what I actually *meant* was . . ." What are some of the reasons for this distinction between what we mean and what we actually say?[14]

[14]For distinction between "speaker analysis" (what was intended) and "discourse analysis" (what was said), see Poythress, *Scottish Journal of Theology* 32(1979):113-37.

We deliberately may try to be evasive, to disguise our feelings and intentions. In the middle of our neighbor's late-evening family movies, we may yawn and say we are sleepy when what we really mean is that we are bored. Such indirection may explain aspects of the Book of Revelation—for instance, the famous beast whose number is 666 is probably a coded reference to the emperor Nero.

We may not be entirely clear ourselves about what we are trying to say. We may even read something we wrote in the past and not find it clear. "I don't know what I was trying to say!"

We may use words incorrectly and think that we are saying one thing when in fact we are saying another.

We may use metaphors or exaggeration so that literally, we do not say "what we mean."

When we move from oral to written communication, the possibility increases that what was said does not equal what was meant. In face to face conversation, one can inquire of the speaker's meaning, and the intent can be clarified. In the case of conversation by letter, the pace and scope of clarification is limited but still possible. But in the case of a book, and especially an ancient one such as the Bible, there cannot be such direct clarification.[15] Discourse is impossible; no questions can be asked of the author; and all nuances of meaning caused by inflection of the voice are lost.

[15]On the distance ("distanciation") caused by reducing material to written form, see Paul Ricoeur, "The Hermeneutical Function of Distanciation," *Exegesis,* ed., Dikran Y. Hadidian, Pittsburgh Theological Monograph Series 21, pp. 297-320; see also "Philosophical Hermeneutics and Biblical Hermeneutics," pp. 321-39.

A document often generates an analytic stance in the reader, whereas the intent of the author may have been toward an emotional or ethical response. The basic intent of the author may not have been to convey information, but the written medium may move us away from what was intended toward "what is said."

In addition to those which arise from author or medium, other factors may create a distinction between what is said and what is meant.[16] Whereas in the world of the author, the "you" who is addressed may have been the Israel of the author's own time, in the world of the text, "you" becomes the reader. When God announces to his depressed people in Babylonian exile, "Fear not, for I have redeemed you . . . I will be with you" (Isa 43:1*b*, 2*a*), modern readers rightfully may feel that the words apply to their own situation. A specific word of address has become a general word.

The meaning of the author may have been obscured through mistranslation. Thus we may not be able to recover what the author actually said, to say nothing of what was intended. For example, consider the various possibilities presented for Job 13:15: "Though he slay me, yet will I trust him" (KJV, expressing trust); "Behold, he will slay me; I have no hope" (RSV, expressing despair); "He may slay me, I'll not quaver" (Anchor Bible, expressing defiance). What the words say in each case is clear; but not all of them express the author's intent!

Level III. What the Author Intended to Accomplish

Behind a specific prohibition or appeal in the Bible, in the author's mind there may have been a more general

[16]See Abraham Cronback, "Unmeant Meanings in Scripture," *HUCA* 36(1965):99-123.

principle upon which it rested. When we think of applying the Bible to life in the present, is it not the more general principle ("spirit") we should grapple with, rather than its specific ancient application ("letter")?

As evidence that the rabbis grasped this distinction, note their understanding of Deuteronomy 15:2. The biblical text specifies that debts are to be cancelled at the arrival of the sabbatical (seventh) year, presumably to prevent the development of economic classes. With the passage of time this prohibition contributed to, rather than alleviated the problems of the poor: Some persons refused to grant loans as the sabbatical year approached. The famous Rabbi Hillel (first cent. A.D.) urged that the rule be ignored, thus placing its "spirit" ahead of its "letter."[17]

The author's intention sometimes may emerge when the words are compared with literature outside the Bible. Consider the famous and often misunderstood guideline called *lex talionis:* "eye for eye, tooth for tooth" (Lev 24:17-21; Deut 19:21; Exod 21:23-25). It has been viewed as being harsh and unyielding, especially when compared with Jesus' suggestion that we turn the other cheek (Matt 5:39; Luke 6:29). But when seen against the background of ancient Near Eastern law codes, in which the punishment could sometimes far exceed the crime, and when the social status of the offender and the offended affected the sentence, (only) an eye for an eye was a great humanitarian advance. Hence the author's egalitarian intent is hidden by the mere words of the text.

Sometimes the author's intention remains obscure, despite our best efforts as interpreters. Consider, as

[17]See "Prosbul," *Encyclopaedia Judaica,* vol. 13 (1971). In actuality, a "loophole" was found, rather than the rule being ignored outright.

examples, the injunctions against bestiality and homosexuality (Lev 18:22-23). The wording is clear, but
what is the purpose of the legislation? Is the writer
convinced that the deity is opposed to such activities as
a matter of principle, or were there practical reasons
for forbidding them? If the latter is the case, were the
reasons so self-evident that, for the initial audience,
there was no need to spell them out? Later interpreters
have suggested (a) Israel's aversion was due to a
suspicion of the Canaanite way of life, just as some
Communist regimes today are suspicious of anything
"Western." (But what would that mean for the
Church's stance in the present, since Canaanite culture
no longer is a competitor?) (b) The practices were part
of Canaanite ritual, and therefore it is cultic bestiality
and homosexuality that are condemned. (But what
would that mean in the present, where those practices
have no religious overtones?) (c) Such activity wasted
semen and thus diminished the growth of Israel at a
time when male children were much needed to clear
the hill country of Palestine.[18] (But what would that
mean for our own culture, where overpopulation is the
problem, rather than the reverse?) Thus, while the
"word" of the text is clear, its "intent" is obscure, as is
evident from the heated debate about homosexuality
in the Church today.

[18]For the Babylonian flood-story as an account of population
control, see Anne Draffkorn Kilmer, "The Mesopotamian Concept
of Overpopulation and Its Solution as Reflected in the Mythology,"
Orientalia 41(1972):160-77. For contrast with ancient Israel, where
after the flood there is a general order to "be fruitful and multiply"
(Gen. 9:1), see Tikva Frymer-Kensky, "The Atrahasis Epic and Its
Significance for Our Understanding of Gen. 1–9," *Biblical Archaeologist* 40(1977):147-55.

Level IV. What the Audience Understood

Since the statements of a modern speaker may not be clear, or because an audience is inattentive, or because a message is heard inevitably through the presuppositions ("glasses") of the hearer, what is attributed to a speaker may be more than, less than, or not at all what actually was said.

While it is true that some Scripture apparently comes to us directly (first person) from the author, much more of it comes to us indirectly. That is, a revered person spoke to a group, and someone within that group then transmitted to others and ultimately to us, what he understood the speaker to have been saying. Thus rather than "I said" and "I did," we usually will find "he said" or "he did." Thus throughout the Pentateuch, Moses is described in the third person, which probably indicates that someone was reporting about him. We cannot even be sure that the reports were formulated by a first-hand observer (such as Joshua). They may have been repeated for generations, until someone gathered and arranged them in their present form.

As a possible illustration of the way first-hand observers may misperceive a biblical speaker's intent, notice Isaiah 7:1-17, in which an oracle of assurance is given in a specific situation. Isaiah says that before the kings of Syria and Israel can attack Judah, they themselves will be attacked by the Assyrians. Thus King Ahaz is not to worry; he is not to enter into an alliance with the Assyrians; he is to trust God to preserve the people as expressed in a traditional liturgical formula "God is with us." Apparently, however, some hearers understood this to be a general assurance of protection regardless of their obedience to God. "God is with us" seems to have been heard as an absolute statement of eternal security. Such a positive, popular use of the phrase seems to appear in 8:9-10, reflecting the same confident mentality against which the prophet spoke. Thus his specific assurances to Ahaz may have been perverted into a general sanction for maintaining the status quo. Does that misunderstanding then cause the prophet to launch into a new, negative oracle, sarcastically using this same phrase? In 8:5-7, he says, in effect, "Yes, I'll be with you . . . like a river drowns its victims!" Has such a change on the prophet's part, prompted by "what the audience heard" as opposed to "what the prophet meant," also resulted in an addition to the last sentence of the unit 7:1-17—"the king of Assyria"—thus transforming the positive oracle into a negative one (along with the addition of 7:18-25)? This illustrates how persons whom we revere as authors of Scripture may have been misunderstood even by their own contemporaries.

We face this type of problem any time we seek to recover the meaning of the prophets whose messages are preserved in the OT. In most cases, it is likely that they did not write down their speeches, and indeed many of them probably could not write. (Note Jeremiah's use of Baruch the Scribe, 36:4.) The oracles thus were remembered, however perfectly or imperfectly, by disciples (Isa 8:16) who handed them down in oral fashion. How well did they understand what they heard? (There is also the subsequent question of how well they remembered what they had understood!) In most cases, "what the prophet said" cannot be disentangled from "what the audience heard." We must be satisfied with the fact that Scripture largely is what was heard, remembered, and handed down, rather than what actually was spoken.

If there is only one generation between a speaker and recorder, then the problem is minimized. But if the initial hearer (H_1) reports to someone else (H_2) what he heard a speaker (S_1) say, then the procedure, with all its precariousness for understanding, is repeated.[19] This can happen a great number of times before the material reaches a written form that is regarded as unchangeable.

Level V. What the Editor (Redactor) Meant

No matter which model we follow for the creation of the Pentateuch in its present form, it is obvious that someone has gathered, selected, and arranged older literature. When previously unrelated materials are combined in sequence, new possibilities for interpretation arise.[20]

For what purpose were the genealogies in Genesis 10:1-32 and 11:10-29 originally compiled? Of that we cannot be sure, but when they are placed in their present literary context, they may serve to illustrate the nature of God's redemptive activity. They bridge the gap between a time of few people (after the flood) and a time of many people (when Abraham was called). Some modern scholars have suggested that through them, the editor(s) of the Bible illustrated the options available to the deity when he moved to choose a special people. Abraham's clan was chosen not because God had few options. Realizing this, the community's gratitude for the deity's graciousness should be enhanced.

[19]See Poythress, esp. pp. 132-34.
[20]See "Redaction-Criticism," *IDBS*.

What is the relationship between "promise" stories and "betrayal" stories? God promises Abraham the land of Canaan (Gen 12:1-9, esp. 12:7); Abraham flees that land and goes down to Egypt (12:10-20). God promises Isaac descendants as numerous as the stars (26:1-5); Isaac gives away his wife through whom the promise could be realized (26:6-11). Are these chronological events, which happened immediately one after the other, as a quick reading of the text might indicate? Or, did these events take place years apart? Did they happen in just this sequence? Were the betrayals a conscious rejection of the promise? These questions cannot be answered easily. What can be said is that the episodes have been placed back to back by the story collectors (editors of Scripture) and that, since the pattern is repeated, there may have been a conscious attempt to make a point: No sooner does God make a promise than the community betrays it. Such an interpretation may be gathered, not from the content of the individual episodes (stories) themselves, but from the editorial "cement" that binds them together.

Level VI. What Later Generations Within the Old Testament Understood

Israel's faith, rather than remaining static (clear from the beginning and consistent throughout), is one of dynamic growth. This took various forms.

Older ideas are expanded. Thus the content of the promise to the Patriarchs grew with the passage of time.[21] Again, the prohibition against lending money to the poor for interest (Exod 22:25) is expanded to all loans within Israel (Deut 23:19-20).

[21]See ch. 4, II.

Older practices are given a new explanation. Some of the dietary laws in Leviticus 11 initially may have forbidden food, such as pork, because it was consumed in the cults of Canaan. Later, when such cults had ceased to be a threat to Israel's religious life, the prohibitions remained in effect but were given a new rationale. During the Exile, they may have served to remind Israel that she was "different," that she was "holy" to the Lord (11:45).[22] In just this fashion her identity was maintained when more traditional ways of doing this became impossible.

Older practices are restricted. Thus places of worship throughout the land (Beersheba, Shechem, Dan, etc.) were shut down at the time of King Josiah, with the sanction of the book of Deuteronomy. The office of priest, apparently once open to members of all the tribes, is progressively restricted to the tribe of Levi (Deuteronomy) and then to the descendants of Aaron (P-code). Presumably then, anyone reading Deuteronomy 33:8, "Give to Levi thy Thummim, and thy Urim to thy godly one," would, in the light of the P-code's restriction, understand the text to mean: "Give to (the priestly part of) Levi thy Thummim."

Older ideas are challenged. Deuteronomy asserts that God's retribution extends across the generations: "visiting the iniquity of the fathers upon the children to the third and fourth generation" (5:9). But Ezekiel (18:1-4) and Jeremiah (31:29-30) stress that each generation is responsible for its own sins. Even Deuteronomy itself shrinks from applying such justice in

[22]Most of Lev. belongs to the collection which the documentary hypothesis assigns to the P-code.

human society (24:16). Later still, The Book of Job will deny that justice is done even for a given generation or individual.

Events in Israel's history are reinterpreted. What was the nature of Israel's relationship to God during the period of wandering in the wilderness? The Pentateuch itself depicts that period as one of repeated rebellion against God (Exod 14:11-12; 16:2-3; 17:1-4; Num 11:1; 14:1-3), and that fact is not lost upon the prophet Ezekiel (20:5-26). Hosea, however, seems to allude to it as an ideal age of obedience (2:15), prior to the fatal temptations that arose in the land of Canaan.

Older ideas are redefined. When the monarchy was introduced to Israel (eleventh cent B.C.), there were those who proposed that it was divinely ordained (1 Sam 9–10). Its continuation in David and Solomon was seen as evidence that the deity had made an unending, unconditional covenant with that line of kings (2 Sam 7). Later, when the monarchy ended at the time of the Babylonian exile, it was proposed that the covenant with David's line had been conditional from the beginning (1 Chr 28:6-7). Deutero-Isaiah then proposes that it has been extended from David's line to the entire people (55:3). Christianity transforms it even more radically by having Jesus, as a descendant of David (Matt 1:1), sit upon a heavenly throne and rule over a spiritual kingdom.

Level VII. New Testament Reinterpretation

On the one hand, apparent departure from the OT meaning may be regarded as the "key" to an OT writer's true intentions. The NT may be seen as containing a fuller, perhaps divinely inspired clarification of the

earlier text. It even may be supposed that the earlier
authors did not grasp the full meaning of what they were
saying. On the other hand, such reinterpretation may be
seen as a historically conditioned attempt by the early
Christian community to make its sacred literature speak
to the present. It may be interesting from the standpoint
of the history of interpretation; it may even be
profound, but it is not necessarily relevant for un-
covering what an OT author "meant."

As an illustration, consider the material that Revelation reuses from the Book of Daniel. In two visions (chs
2 and 7), the author of Daniel describes four world
empires, stretching from the Exile (587 B.C.) to the
restoration of the sanctuary in Jerusalem (165 B.C.?).
The fourth beast with ten horns in chapter 7 appears to
be Greece. (Compare 8:21—Greece is mentioned by
name.) But the author of 2 Esdras (also called 4 Ezra)
wants the comforting words of Daniel to be meaningful
to his own day, when Rome has replaced Greece as the
persecutor of the Jews. Hence he says, "The eagle . . .
represents the fourth kingdom in the vision seen by your
brother Daniel. But he was not given the interpretation
which I am now giving you" (12:11-12 NEB). The
author apparently goes on to refer to Rome, having
admitted his realization that this is not what the author
of Daniel had in mind. The author of Revelation,
evidently following the lead of 2 Esdras, also sees a beast
arising from the sea (13:1-4). Like Daniel's fourth beast,
it has ten horns. And as in Daniel (ch 14), God's justice
will be instituted on earth following the beast's
destruction. But unlike Daniel and like 2 Esdras, this
beast apparently is to be identified with Rome. Daniel
has been reinterpreted.

Level VIII. Traditional Understandings
in Other Than Canonical Literature

How has a given text come to be interpreted within the postbiblical Believing Communities? Such traditional understandings may have become so self-evidently "right" within our particular group that we would not be aware that they do not agree with any or all of the previously mentioned levels of meaning.

The origins of such traditional meanings include *ancient versions of the Bible*. The manner in which a particular ancient translation rendered a given text was a reflection of the prevailing understanding of those who produced it, and perhaps of the larger community to which they belonged. It subsequently may shape the way the community continues to understand that text and indeed, may become the authority for that understanding.

What is the nature of the last part of the promise to Abraham in Genesis 12:1-3? Does it promise that his clan will be a source of blessing for others, or merely that others will pray to be blessed in the same way? The Hebrew text is ambiguous, but the Septuagint (Greek translation), in the third century B.C., believes it is the former. One could say that the Egyptian Jewish community (where the Septuagint was produced) retained an openness to others which supported its interpretation of Genesis 12:1-3; or one could argue that the translators were inspired by God to clarify the proper understanding of this crucial but ambiguously worded text (progressive-revelation position).

In addition to ancient versions of Scripture the *opinions of the spiritual fathers* of a particular Believing Community may come to be regarded as "the" meaning of a text.

Who are the "sons of God" who have intercourse with the "daughters of men" in Genesis 6:1-4? Although some ancient interpreters (as well as "conservative" Protestant writers from the nineteenth cent. onward) have taken this to be a reference to "fallen angels," Augustine understood it to be a reference to tyrannical local rulers who seized their female subjects for sexual use. (He pointed out, quite correctly, that some ancient rulers were flattered by being called the offspring of God.) This then became a traditional Medieval interpretation.

In Genesis 38:8-10, we are told that Onan, during intercourse with his deceased brother's wife, "spilled the semen on the ground" and that "what he did was displeasing in the sight of the Lord, and he slew him." As early as Augustine, this passage was understood to be a divine sanction against masturbation. Indeed, the activity itself has come to be called onanism. However, this traditional interpretation misunderstands the contextual reason Onan was condemned—because he would not produce offspring for his brother.[23]

We turn now from the Western (Roman) Fathers to the interpretations of those in the Eastern Church. What are we to make of the plural pronouns in Genesis 1:26? The deity remarks, "Let us make man in our image, after our likeness." The early Greek Fathers tended to see this as a reference to the Second Person of the Trinity (the preexistent Christ), and most of the Church subsequently came to see it in the same way.[24] While most Christian readers in the present would assume this

[23]See "Levirate Law," *IDB*.

[24]Origen (3rd cent.), "Against Celsus," vol. 37, *Ante-Nicene Fathers*, 4, 560a; also Basil of Caesarea (4th cent.), "Homily 9," vol. 46, *Fathers of the Church*, pp. 147-50.

to be the self-evident meaning of the text, from the point of view of modern scholarship, it has no validity.

I turn now to an illustration from rabbinic literature. The eighth commandment (Exod 20:15) reads, "You shall not steal." Christian interpreters have come to understand that it prohibits the theft of physical property. For most of us, that "self-evidently" is the "right" meaning. In rabbinic literature, however, it is assumed to refer to persons: "You shall not kidnap."[25] And the immediate context of the verse can be seen to support that understanding: The commandments before and after it (adultery and false witness) are crimes against persons, not property. Furthermore, it could be argued that theft of property may be covered by the last commandment ("You shall not covet . . . anything that is your neighbor's").

Level IX. What the Text Means to the Modern Reader— "What It Means to Me"

Each text, of course, will have some meaning to every interpreter in the present (unless one says, "I don't know what it's all about"). It is important to realize, however, that the present meaning to an individual may not coincide with any of the aforementioned levels of meaning. It can result from any of the reasons that have been mentioned previously: disregard of the context of the passage; lack of knowledge of the historical setting; mistranslation; preconceived notions ("glasses") and personal needs.

[25]The verb used *(ganab)* can refer to either kind of "theft." For the above interpretation, see the *Mechilta* (Tannaitic Midrash on Exod.).

It is crucial to ask, What is the importance of this level of meaning? It could be argued that (a) since we cannot be sure what the biblical author meant to say; and (b) since what the author actually said is sometimes unclear; and (c) since the words, once uttered, take on a life of their own apart from their original historical context; and (d) since texts were reinterpreted within Scripture itself and by revered leaders of the postbiblical community, perhaps guided by the Holy Spirit—then we can believe that the Holy Spirit continues to guide the present community, or even individuals, toward the creative interpretation and application of Scripture.

This level of meaning is likely to be both presupposed and encouraged by casual reading of the Bible. Each night a few verses may be read, quickly, often with some printed devotional commentary such as *Guideposts* or *The Upper Room.* The same level of meaning may be created in Bible "study" groups, where a text is read, just as it is, with no attention to the author's historical setting, possible textual problems, or its literary context. The assumption seems to be, "Just read the Bible: It'll speak to you!"

Such an approach to the Bible is similar to recent literary criticism, especially as applied to some modern poetry.[26] In this approach, a poet need not be making a clearly defined personal statement, and therefore our goal is not to recover "what the author meant." Rather, good poetry may, or even should be impersonal and open to various understandings. There is no one legitimate reading, but various plausible, sensitive interpretations,

[26]See Hirsch, *Validity in Interpretation.*

depending upon the way it strikes the individual reader, with his or her own unique background, presuppositions, and needs. The question is thus no longer, What did the author of this poem intend to say? but, How do you understand it? What is your reading?

When applied to the Bible, such an approach, while laudable from the point of view of moving beyond "what the text meant" to "what it means" in the present, encounters a few difficulties.

One may doubt whether such a modern approach to art and literature should be read back into an earlier time. Not long ago, artists and poets *did* try, and successfully, to convey specific ideas. We may assume that this was the case with the biblical authors as well, even if the recovery of their intent is exceedingly difficult.

"What the text meant" and "what it means (to me)" are combined into one step in interpretation. It may seem that they are the same; that the transition from-then-to-now is automatic and thus that study of context, original situation, and so on, is irrelevant.[27] The *last* question has become the *first* question.

Such an interpretative approach usually individualizes the text. Whereas it initially may have been addressed to the community and its socio-economic and political problems, the text now is made to apply to me and to my personal problems. As an illustration,

[27]Speaking of this approach as applied to modern literature, W. K. Wimsatt, Jr., remarks, "The Affective Fallacy is a confusion between the poem and its results (what it *is* and what it *does*). . . . It begins by trying to derive the standard of criticism from the psychological effect of the poem and ends in impressionism and relativism. The outcome . . . is that the poem itself, as an object of special critical judgment, tends to disappear" (*The Verbal Icon* [Lexington: University of Kentucky Press, 1954], p. 21).

consider the following advice about the way we might approach the story of Jesus' healing the paralytic (Mark 2:1-12): "The distance [between then and now?] collapses. . . . It becomes necessary to ask how the text resonates in us as we ask, who is the paralytic in you? . . . who is the 'scribe' in you? . . . What would it be like to . . . move to the healing source? That, after all, is what the story's about, isn't it?"[28] No, we must reply, that is not the story's clear meaning in any of the previous nine levels of interpretation. It becomes so only in this modern application of the text to one's psychological state.

Such an approach may allow one's preconceived notions ("glasses") to have maximum effect upon interpretation. Each interpreter may be encouraged to hear what he or she is predisposed to hear. Indeed, the way the reader "feels" about the text becomes the crucial point.

Insofar as this approach leads to individual interpretation, it diminishes the Bible as the community's book. Rather than the text being directed to the community's problems and being interpreted by the community as a hedge against individual subjectivism, the individual now becomes the ultimate addressee and authority in interpretation. All communal coherence is threatened.

[28]Wink, *The Bible in Human Transformation*, pp. 55, 56, 58; for analysis, see Elizabeth Schussler Fiorenza, "'For the Sake of Our Salvation . . .': Biblical Interpretation as Theological Task," *Sin, Salvation, and the Spirit*, ed. Durken, p. 24.

THE PRESENT:
POSSIBLE APPLICATION
OF SELECTED TEXTS

CHAPTER FOUR

Now that the reader has gained some understanding of possible ways in which the Pentateuchal materials were gathered (ch 1) and has reflected upon some assumptions that might be operative when it is studied (chs 2 and 3), we now may inquire as to the way this knowledge can shape the application of selected texts in the present.

Given the limitations of space, the number of texts must be strictly limited. The following criteria have governed my selection:

1. A text from the "prehistoric" (perhaps some would call it the unhistoric) period (Gen 1–11), collectively known as the Primeval History—The Creation Account—Genesis 1:1–2:4a;

2. The text that bridges the gap between the "prehistoric" and the patriarchal (some would say semihistoric) periods—The Bridge Between the Primeval and the Patriarchal—Genesis 12;

3. Several texts which relate to a single theme—The Naming of Isaac—Genesis 17:15-22; 18:1-16; 21:1-7;

4. A familiar text—The Near-Sacrifice of Isaac—Genesis 22;

5. Ethical guidelines—The Ten Commandments—
Exodus 20:1-17;

6. An unfamiliar, seemingly irrelevant text—The
Necessity for Tassels on Garments—Numbers 15:37-41.

Of the texts I have chosen, the widely used COCU
lectionary contains the following: Genesis 1:1–2:3;
12:1-8; 18:1-14; 22:1-18; and Exodus 20:1-17.

From the models for the formation of the Pentateuch
previously presented, for the sake of concise discussion I
have chosen the documentary hypothesis for my point of
departure. It is to be hoped that readers who do not
share that perspective will find other aspects of the
discussion helpful.

I. The Creation Account—Genesis 1:1–2:4a

Background Information

Where does the story end? Since the present chapter
divisions are Medieval, we cannot rely upon them to tell
us when a literary unit is complete. Instead, we must rely
upon recent English translations. The NEB places
1:1–2:4a together, ending the story with, "This is the
story of the making of heaven and earth when they were
created." The same division is found in TEV, which
ends, "And that is how the universe was created" (see
also NJV). We thus find a fittingly worded conclusion to
a completed story.

Who were the editors of this story? Although parts of
the story may be very old, its concerns and expressions
relate it to other materials associated with the P
(Priestly) Code: reference to the deity as "God"
(*'elohim*); concern with lists and order (six days on
which things happen); the characteristic expressions—

"These are the generations" (2:4; 5:1; 6:9; 10:1; 11:10), "Be fruitful and multiply" (1:28; 8:17; 9:1), "In his own image" (1:27; 5:3; 9:6).

What was the situation at the time the text took its final shape? If the text was finalized at the hands of the Priestly Writers, then it was addressed to an Israel in Babylonian exile, or to those who remained behind in the ravaged home-country, or to those who returned home to find their world forever changed. There had been death, exile, and divisiveness (evident in Neh), as well as defection to the religion of the prevailing military power, Babylonia (evident in Isa 40–55). The religious practices which formerly had given identity and had told one what it meant to be a member of the elect of God—rule by a Davidic descendant (2 Sam 7), worship in Jerusalem only (Deut 12), the great festivals (Deut 26)—were now difficult or impossible to maintain. Indeed, the question asked of Ezekiel, "How then can we live?" (33:10) was an urgent one.

What questions does the text try to answer? The major ones seem to be: (a) What divine force is in control of the world, given the fact that it has been dominated militarily by the Babylonians and then by the Persians? (b) How does Israel remember who it is, in a world that seeks to deprive it of its former identity?

In response to the question of control, we should not be surprised to find Genesis 1 mounting a sustained attack upon polytheism (the worship of non-Israelite gods).

In the Babylonian-created epic (entitled *Enuma Elish*), the primeval sea, called Tiamat (a form of *tiamtu* ["sea"]), is subdued by the national god Marduk. Creation thus results from a cosmic struggle. By contrast, Genesis 1 reduces the "deep" *(tehom)* to

impersonal matter, effortlessly shaped by a God who
was sovereign from the beginning.

In a Sumerian creation epic, it is the wind god Enlil
who brings order out of chaos. But in Genesis 1, the
wind also is reduced to an impersonal "thing" which
does Yahweh's bidding.

Light is created before the luminaries—before the sun
god, in particular. Yahweh then separates light from
darkness. They are not manifestations of the twin
dualistic gods whom the Persians worshiped.

The earth is commanded to bring forth vegetation.
But it is a mere object, not the body of an ancient
goddess who must be worshiped in order to bestow her
blessings upon humankind.

The sun, the moon, and the stars also are objects
created by Yahweh. They are not powerful gods, each
with a sacred text, rituals, temple, and priesthood of its
own, as in Mesopotamia and Canaan.

The animals, regarded by some of Israel's neighbors
as the embodiment of divine forces, are nothing of the
sort. They are mere creatures, and at Yahweh's word
alone do they "multiply, and fill the earth."

To sum up, Israel's neighbors, and now some of its
own people, have been attributing deity to inanimate
objects, to mere "birdies, beasties, and fishes."[1] Harvey
Cox is right when he speaks of this passage as a form of
"atheistic propaganda" (from a non-Israelite point of
view), since it refuses to see nature as alive with divine
forces.[2] Humans, rather than bowing down to the
created order, are given dominion over it (v 26).

[1] I owe this formulation to James Sanders.
[2] H. G. Cox, *The Secular City* (New York: Macmillan Paperbacks,
1965), p. 23.

In response to the problem of "remembering who we are," it is not surprising to find Genesis 1 reaching its conclusion at the establishment of the sabbath. It is so important as a time for reflection and remembering (Exod 20:11) that God initiated it in the very beginning and even observes it himself.

Assumptions in the Move from Past to Present

• The meaning is not self-evident, since there are arguments as to the way it relates to the present (ch 2, I).
• Since this is a familiar text, I must beware of deciding too quickly that I know what it means (ch 2, II, A).
• As a member of the Believing Community, I cannot read this merely as a report of the thinking of ancient Israel. I must wrestle, in community, about its possible meaning today (ch 2, III, B).
• The story is likely to have a deeper purpose than that of simply listing a sequence of events. I must search for theological meaning (ch 2, III, C).
• It is critical study that produced the background information above, which was crucial in the recovery of the text's overall meaning (ch 2, III, D).
• I will concentrate upon the overall meaning of the literary unit, rather than try to draw significance from its smaller parts (ch 3, I, C).

A Suggested Direction in the Present

Any theological discussion of our current ecological crisis must be informed by and respond to the position of historian Lynn White, Jr. His thesis is that science and technology are largely Western in origin and development because they are the heirs of Western religion (Judeo-Christianity). By this he means that biblical teleology, with its idea of God's goal-directed history, gave rise to the idea of inevitable human progress. Furthermore, he says, Christianity, in its Western (Latin) form, is uniquely human-centered: It insists that humans were the goal of creation, and yet it sets them apart from the other creatures as alone having infinite value in God's eyes. These two faiths, says White, "not only established a dualism of man and nature but also insisted that it is God's will that man exploit nature for his proper ends."[3] We cannot deny that many Judeo-Christians have had such an exploitative approach to nature or that a reading of the Bible may have played a role in it. However, I suggest that a proper reading of Genesis 1 could have had the opposite effect.

Does the fact that humans are given dominion over nature (v 26) mean that they are free to exploit it as they please, to use it up merely for their own gain and comfort? That would seem to be a traditional under-standing, and perhaps it has played a major role in the current crisis. But does not such a reading ignore the literary context and historical background of the verse? Does not such exploitation of nature indicate a surrender to the very idolatry against which the passage speaks? A god is that to which one owes ultimate allegiance; that which is desired above all else; that which determines one's thoughts and actions. The real problem with the Canaanite fertility cults was not that they asserted that there was a "spook" up in the sky named Baal, in competition with Yahweh, but that they deified the processes of nature. They made "the good life," the acquisition of "things," the expansion of the Gross National Product, into a god worthy of human dedication. Indeed, it was a god whose blessings were

[3]*Science* 155(March 1967):1203-1207.

worthy of acquisition, even through human sacrifice. In those days, such sacrifice involved burning a person alive; now it involves tolerating smog and dangerous products lest "the old economy" suffer a setback. In our consumer-oriented society, have we indeed obtained dominion over nature, or is it the reverse? Has our current crisis resulted from our hearing Genesis 1, or from our *not* having heard it?

For nature to exercise dominion over humans (the reverse of our passage), it would be necessary that most of our activities be oriented with respect to it and that our lives be dedicated to the acquisition of its blessings. Is not true dominion over nature the ability to refuse the tyranny of "things," to refuse them for other values (or gods)? Is not true freedom to be found in the realization that "a man's life does not consist in the abundance of his possessions" (Luke 12:15)? Does not true freedom lie in being free of the alleged gods of sea, sky, and earth—free to find one's meaning and identity elsewhere, in the One who is God alone?

This polemical thrust of the text points toward the conclusion of the creation story: the setting aside of the sabbath day. Humans, created in God's image, should worship the true God, but they will fail to do so unless there is a day set aside for communal and individual reflection.

Possible False Directions

1. "Let's begin with some contemporary problem that this text can be made to address, such as creation versus evolution or the equality of male and female." Problem: These are modern agendas, rather than those of the text. They ignore the central thrust of the story.

2. "Let's begin with some phrase 'I can do something with,' such as 'God saw that everything was good.' Doesn't that include human sexuality, which our society tries to repress?" Problem: God's statement of approval, though important, is not the thrust of the story.

3. "God is the source of the whole creative process."[4] It is doubtful that anyone in the ancient world would deny this; however, it is a modern assertion. The ancient question may have been, "What/Who is God, and what is the appropriate response?"

4. "The reading of the story further points toward the new creation and restoration of the divine image which had been defaced by sin."[5] This is not part of the thrust of the story, although it may appear so when the Church pairs it with NT texts in the lectionary for Holy Week. Thus the Church calendar becomes one's interpretive "glasses."

II. The Bridge Between the Primeval and the Patriarchal—Genesis 12

Background Information

There are translation problems. The major difference, when various English translations are compared, is to be found in verse 3. The RSV reads, "By you all the families of the earth will bless themselves." But we are alerted to a problem by the presence of a footnote: "Or, 'in you all the families of the earth will be blessed.'" The main text is not especially clear, but its intent is the same as NEB: "All the families on earth will pray to be

[4]Reginald H. Fuller, *Preaching the New Lectionary* (Collegeville, Md.: Liturgical Press, 1974), p. 21.
[5]*Ibid.*

blessed as you are blessed." Does God single Israel out for an isolated blessing which will leave others "green with envy" (RSV, NEB)? Or are they singled out to be an instrument for the blessing of others (RSV footnote)?

We must go to the commentaries for clarification, where we soon discover that the problem is caused by an ambiguous form of the Hebrew verb (the *Niph'al* form). It can be either passive ("be blessed") or reflexive ("bless themselves" = "pray to be blessed"). It is unclear how we are to translate the given verb. How do we decide, especially when the commentaries may disagree?[6]

Two methods of inquiry are open to us. First we ask, is the promise to Abraham repeated anywhere else, and if so, is that language more clear? It is repeated in 22:18 and 26:4, where the commentaries tell us that another verbal form, clearly reflexive, is used (the *Hithpa'el* form, which is clearly "pray to be blessed"). Should we not therefore, it is argued, choose the same meaning in 12:3? Before we accept this logical argument, we must ask ourselves, Were there, in the early period, differing ideas about the destiny of Israel?

So our first method of getting at the meaning of the verb may have led us to a dead end. But there is a second. Does the wider context of the passage shed any light on the author's intended meaning? Does the material preceding chapter 12 have any bearing on the reason Abraham was called, at least in the opinion of those who arranged the material in this sequence? My

[6]Gerhard von Rad, *Genesis*, reads it as a passive ("will be blessed"); E. A. Speiser, *Genesis*, Anchor Bible Series (New York: Doubleday & Co., 1964), reads it as a reflexive ("will pray to be blessed").

thought is that the answer is yes and that it supports the reading in the RSV footnote.

Who were the editors of this story? We note the use of the proper name of the deity, Yahweh ("the Lord"), a characteristic of the Yahwist. In verse 6 we note the term "Canaanites," another J characteristic. And when we turn to the commentaries, we find agreement at this point.

What was the situation at the time the text took its final shape? When did J live? What was the social-political-economic-religious situation of the time? And how does that help us to understand the passage?

There is a majority conviction that J lived at the end of David's reign. If so, it was a time of great economic prosperity, political expansion, artistic and literary accomplishment, and human achievement and self-confidence. The future seemed open, and the young nation of Israel seemed capable of achieving whatever image or goal it set for itself. Is it to be an economic power? A powerful military force? A religious community? Now is the time to decide, when there is vitality waiting to be channeled, while everyone waits to see what the energetic new king, Solomon, will accomplish. Otherwise put: J may be in a position to suggest an identity, to mold the self-understanding of his people.

But there is another factor. Self-confidence and achievement may breed a contempt for religion, suggesting that it is not God in whom we should trust, but ourselves. The old stories of God's promises and activities may come to be viewed as pious superstition, which "Man come of age" no longer can believe. J, then, might well be concerned to point to God's activity in the present through ordinary-appearing events. When J sets out to address these problems, he reinterprets older material, and that brings us to the next question.

How has earlier tradition possibly been modified in this version of the promise? The account of the promise found in Genesis 12:1-3 is not the only account in the Pentateuch, and indeed it differs from several others: while 12:1-3 mentions offspring and blessing, some list offspring and land (Gen 13:14-17; 26:3-4; 28:3-4; 35:11-12); others, only land (12:7; 15:7, 18; 24:7); and still others, only offspring (15:5; 46:3). Given the fact that J is a collector and editor, more than an author, these variations cannot be attributed to literary whim. They are sacred traditions, handed down in varying forms, ever in the process of growth.

The question then must be asked, In Genesis 12:1-3, in what sense is J merely passing on an old tradition, and in what sense (if any) is he innovatively speaking to the problems of his own age? We are on very uncertain ground here, but it would seem logical to suppose that the earliest form of the promise would concern offspring, since this is a near-universal human concern. Also ancient, but less basic as a concern, would be the desire for a dwelling place. Indeed, Deuteronomy mentions the patriarchal promise only as one of land (6:23; 26:3; etc.). Furthermore, the promise to give the land to Abraham and his descendants would have been regarded as fulfilled when he arrived there, many centuries before the time of J. And yet in J, it is clear that the promise of land applies to the conquest of Canaan under Joshua. The promise has been extended and given a new meaning, apparently as part of J's creative theological genius: God's promises may not be exhausted by their original application. Thus J seeks to demonstrate that God is still at work. A response to the deity is in order, at the very moment when identity is in the process of formation.

The third element of the promise in verses 1-3—blessing in relation to others—is extremely rare (Gen 18:18; 28:14). There is no reason to suppose that it is as old as the other two (land and offspring): It is not as basic to human existence, and it presupposes the establishment of a successful society and considerable time for reflection. This blessing, therefore, may be J's own suggestion as to Israel's identity: That it should become basically not an economic or political power, not an exclusivistic religious group, but a community that would be a blessing to all the families of the earth.

What is its literary form? Among the various types defined by literary critics, "saga" perhaps best describes Genesis 12 and the material that follows. Briefly, the saga is an oral, poetic narrative, in which the leading character(s) may represent groups. Abraham thus represents Israel. A saga is told in order to link the hearer with the group and with the events being related, which may be partly historical and partly imaginative. The saga has a certain detachment from precise time and space: We are not told when Abraham went to Egypt, where he settled, or even the name of the pharaoh. All that is of minor importance. There is a certain freedom in shaping the material, and sagas often begin with the formula, "And it happened after these things that (so-and-so took place)."

How is the story related to its larger context? If a single verse cannot be understood apart from its context without the risk of doing violence to it, could not the same be true of an entire story (or chapter)? Has J joined his stories in a random fashion, or is there an orderliness, a progression, from one chapter to the next? Is it possible that the clue to J's opinion as to the calling of Abraham is found in chapters 1–11? I suggest that these chapters consist of a series of originally unrelated stories.

Everyone knew an old story about a man and a woman in a garden: "humankind" *('adam)* and Eve. It was an entertaining tale that explained how we all got here, why we must work, and so on.

They also knew a story about two brothers, one a farmer-blacksmith, Cain, and the other a shepherd, Abel. It was a drama about fights between farmers and shepherds, which often took place, and the idea that God preferred animal sacrifice to grain. No one yet had suggested that the shepherd and the farmer were the sons of Adam and Eve. Have you ever wondered where Adam and Eve were, while the murder was being done? They appear nowhere, perhaps because it was once an independent story. Note also that there must have been other people around, for Cain goes off and marries a wife. Only when the two accounts are joined, does this problem emerge.

There was also an old story about "sons of God" who married "daughters of men" (Gen 6), which may have explained the giants that people said once lived on the earth. At any rate, there were some huge tombs which suggested that there had been giants in the land.[7]

The people knew a story about a flood that had destroyed the world. It was a story known also to the Sumerians, the Assyrians, and the Babylonians. Each told the story so that one of their boys was the hero, their

[7]See "Dolmens," *IDB* and *IDBS*.

gods were the cause, and the ark came to rest just down the road, where everyone could see it.

They also knew a story about a huge tower that had fallen into ruin (Gen 11), and which explained, they said, how people became scattered all over the earth and spoke so many languages.

And not only were all these stories unrelated, they were not told as "history" in the strict sense of the term. Where did Adam and Eve live? Where did Cain kill Abel? Where did Noah live? All this is set down without concern for "when" and "where." Only when we come to the life of Abraham are we dealing with events which seem more clearly to have a historical foundation.

What questions does the text try to answer? The J theologians took these old, familiar, unrelated stories and put them together, not because someone needed to collect and publish them, but because they could be used as "sermon illustrations." They make vivid the beliefs that J wanted the people of his day to accept. They are true, not so much historically as theologically. They capture the nature of humans, illustrate their pride, make clear the difficulties God faced in trying to deal with them.

What does the story look like, as J gets it all together? It begins something like this, or so it appears in the larger context. Is the world in which we live ideal? Is it as God created it or intended it? No, and the fault lies in the human will. Humans do not like to have boundaries placed upon them. They desire knowledge ("the tree of knowledge") and ignore the consequences of obtaining it. The serpent represents the ego, which will not let humans accept the fact that they are creatures and accountable for their actions. Adam, meaning human-kind, is the essence, the illustration of every person.

The J theologians use other ancient stories to illustrate the excesses of human beings, once they reject their creaturehood and decide that they are free to do as they please. He tells of Cain and Abel, making them the children of "Adam" and Eve. Man will kill his own brother in an argument over religion; he will take unlimited revenge upon those who harm him (thus the Song of Lamech, an old tribal boast); indeed, "Every imagination . . . of his heart was . . . evil" (6:5).

It may be suggested by J that God continues to care for creation, and this is illustrated with other well-known stories. The deity protects Cain. The human race is allowed to continue (i.e., "Adam" has other sons and daughters). The human life span is reduced in order to limit the power to do evil (thus the "giant" stories are reinterpreted). Humans are punished with near-total destruction, but the righteous are saved for a new beginning (the flood). The nations are separated by language, as a limitation upon their accomplishments.

Yet J may be suggesting that none of this works. Humans remain as prideful, as stubborn, as violent, as unresponsive as before. They have not learned from example, from exhortation, from threat, or from alienation. All this is true, and we know it. It is true, and true for us. The stories have been made to serve a new theological purpose. "They never were, but they always are."

By the end of chapter 11, one may suppose the message to be that God has almost reached the end of his rope. Is there any other way to get through to humans? God, J may be implying, tries one last desperate gamble by selecting one small family, in the hope that it will

respond and be a model and witness to others. Will an
Israel succeed where all else has failed?

Assumptions in the Move from Past to Present

• That the promise originally extended to Abraham has
been renewed to his descendants and that J can apply it
even to the settlement in Canaan, hundreds of years
later—this is the precedent whereby we may believe that
it can be extended to us in the present. The Bible itself has
established a basic rule for application (see ch 3, VI).

• It is the larger literary context that illuminates the
reason this story was placed exactly where it is, and this
gives insight into the mind of the collectors. And this is
the level of meaning that addresses a persistent problem
of the Believing Communities in the present (ch 3, V).

• If "saga" is an accurate description of this type of story,
then we should try to use the text with that ancient
purpose in mind (ch 2, IV, B). We thus will understand
Abraham as more than an ancient character: He is Israel
personified. His problems, doubts, and hopes are
perennial ones. They help us to understand ourselves as
members of the community.

A Suggested Direction in the Present

Will Israel succeed? Are her daughter institutions, the
Synagogue and the Church, viable institutions? Realis-
tically, is it all worthwhile? These are debatable issues in
view of the fact that humans, including members of the
Believing Communities, do not seem to have changed
much in four thousand years. We still believe that
knowledge is its own reward, that fruit from the tree of
knowledge may be taken without regard for consequences. We would master the atom, harness the
weather, tamper with genetic codes, all in the absence of a

value-system to direct us. We carry out medical experiments on human patients, even if it kills them, and justify the results as "knowledge." We still kill, not with a stick as Cain may have done, but with napalm. And we may do so, now as then, in an argument over religion (holy war, the Muslims call it). We have brought the world to the brink of destruction, not with a flood, but with nuclear and biological weapons, or more inevitably with pollution.

It is a very discouraging world in which we live, but one in which hope is still possible . . . at least, if the Story is to be believed. There is immediate hope because there still are "Abrahams"—people who are willing to obey God and to pass on the goals of the faith to the next generation. There is ultimate hope, because God kept the promise even when Abraham had betrayed it: Sarah was returned because God desired that there be an Israel. Even the instrument of redemption may need to be redeemed, and that, says the Torah, God has done repeatedly.

Possible False Directions

"Abraham as the paradigm of faith." This emphasis is found in the NT and throughout Christian thought. Such a point of view is encouraged by modern lectionaries which end the story too soon, selecting only 12:1-8 (COCU) or 12:1-4a (Roman Catholic). When the entire context is studied, the opposite portrait emerges and God, rather than Abraham, becomes the hero. The issue is not so much, "What kind of person was Abraham?" but "What was God trying to do?" The text must not be humanized and a moral lesson drawn (ch 2, IV, F; IV, B).

III. The Naming of Isaac—
Genesis 17:15-22; 18:1-16; 21:1-7

Background Information

Who were the editors of these stories? Genesis 17:15-22, like the rest of the chapter, is assignable to the Priestly Source. Note the concern with specific age (v 1), the designation of the deity as "God Almighty" (v 1) and as "God" *('elohim)* throughout. Genesis 18:1-16 belongs to the Yahwist source. Note the appearance of deity in human form (vv 2, 8—the deity even eats), and the designation "the Lord" (vv 1, 14). Genesis 21:1-7 contains a mixture of sources. Verse 1 (and possibly 2*a*) belong to J; verses 2*b*-5 seem to be P; and verses 6-7, like much of the rest of the chapter, may be E.

What was the situation at the time the texts took their final shape? Since the situation of the various sources has been discussed, it need not be repeated here. It is curious to note that the E account seems more ancient than the J, or at least less theologically shaped.

How is the situation addressed by these texts? Perhaps we should begin by saying that the name Isaac in Hebrew appears to mean "He laughs." The name itself does not tell us who is laughing. But we can guess. Many names in the Bible tell us something about God (e.g., Joshua means "Yahweh saved"). Possibly, then, Isaac originally meant "He (God) laughs"—that is, looks with favor upon the birth of the child. And this is very close to the sentiment expressed in perhaps the earliest mention of the name, Genesis 21:6. Sarah rejoices and says, "God has made laughter for me; everyone who hears [of the birth] will laugh [rejoice with] me." In this popular version, the subject who laughs possibly has been changed from God to the wife and her friends.

But this is not the only way the name was explained, as we see in 18:9-15. Here both parents are involved. We are told that they are old, but not how old. When the divine guests announce that Sarah will have a child, she laughs—not out of impiety, since she does not know the divine nature of the guests, but because of their ignorance of human biology! After all, at her age? Those who later heard this telling of the story would have given it a wider and religious interpretation. The human race still continued many of its old practices despite the witness of Israel. Indeed, such abuses were widespread even within the community itself! Had the idea that Israel could be "a blessing" been a mistake of Abraham's imagination? Or would the promise yet be realized? Was not such an unlikely prospect enough to make the thoughtful person smile, or even laugh? It was as likely to happen as an old woman giving birth! And yet, the story goes on, the next spring, it happened!

Thus far, the accounts have been told us by the earlier schools of theologians, J and E. But there was yet another version of the giving of the name—this one preserved by the very last school of theologians, P. They write during or just after the Exile when the remnants of Israel were unlikely candidates to be a blessing to all the families of the earth. They are few, demoralized, and ridiculed by others. Could anything have seemed more ridiculous than those ancient promises to the Patriarchs, or the hope that Israel would yet realize its destiny? So P's version of the story fits the needs of the hour. We find it in chapter 17. We are specifically told that Abraham is 99 years old and Sarah, 90. The story is made to sound as impossible as one could imagine. And there is God, still promising a son, despite the odds. Abraham, unlike Sarah in the earlier version, now knows precisely to whom he is talking. When he hears the vision of an Israel-to-be, he "falls on his face," a term which usually means "to worship." But just when we expect him to praise God for the vision, we find that Abraham has fallen on his face for another reason—he collapses with laughter! That there might still be an Isaac, that the promise still might be realized, Abraham is depicted as suggesting, is about the most ridiculous idea he has ever heard! And God responds, "Very well! You must name the child for the attitude you have displayed. You laughed, so name him 'He laughs.'"

Assumptions in the Move from Past to Present

• I need not worry about these different explanations for the origin of the name. I need not try to harmonize them so that all the tensions disappear. The Bible contains ancient traditions that differ, and more than one point of view (ch 2, III, E).

• I must look beyond statements of "fact" to a deeper meaning—to the story's identity-forming and identity-sustaining qualities (ch 2, III, C).

• It is only through critical study that I have been able to understand the way changing historical circumstances might have contributed to these varying accounts of the name (ch 2, III, D).

• I should use the material according to its original intent—as a story with which our existence is bound up (ch 2, IV, B).

• This is a story about the community, rather than about individuals within it (ch 2, IV, C).

A Suggested Direction in the Present

Members of the Synagogue and Church today can appreciate the skepticism of Abraham and Sarah and can understand the despair and doubt of some of the generations that came after them. Even as we hear the promise read in the worship service, we may wonder secretly if the kingdom of God ever will be realized. To be sure, great progress has been made. The vision, once limited to Palestine, now influences all the civilizations of the world. For example, slavery, at one time almost universal, now has been abolished. The Church played a major role in that victory, but some elements of the Church supported slavery to the end. Women, once treated as physical property, are being recognized as fully human. Church leaders have exercised some influence here, but not enough and far too late. The Church has cared for the sick and fed the hungry, at least part of the time. It often has stood against unjust governments, although some clergy will support the state, or say nothing, regardless of the injustice.

The Church, then, is still on its journey, still wandering in the wilderness somewhere between the land of Egypt and the land of the promise. And those of us who are discouraged that change comes so slowly can understand why our spiritual fathers preserved the story of Isaac's birth. We, like they, can see the present reflected in it. It is a true story of the failure and of the hope of the Church. In telling the story, in remembering, hope is created, because God is remembered as faithful. The birth of Isaac, and his name, forever must remind us that we laughed at God, but that the deity has kept and will keep the promise.

Possible False Directions

Abraham as a model of hospitality: "It was not the last time that a generous spirit has found that he has 'entertained angels unaware' (Heb 13:2)."[8] While this statement may be true, it seeks to draw a moral, or a least a lesson in manners, which was not a deliberate point of the biblical story. It not only moralizes, but does so from an incidental in the text. For the same reason, this passage is paired in the lectionary with Luke 10:38-42: "The connection with the Gospel may be . . . in the picture of Abraham as a combination of Martha (v 6, 'Abraham hastened') and of Mary (Abraham stands in silence while his guests eat, v 8). Abraham emerges as a model of both service and patience."[9]

IV. The Near-Sacrifice of Isaac—Genesis 22

Background Information

Where does the story end? We may delete verses 20-24 from the main narrative, since (a) the introductory words ("after these things") set these verses apart in time; and (b) this is a standard phrase apparently used by biblical editors to link stories together (15:1; 22:1; 48:1). Thus the genealogy originally will have been separate, with a purpose of its own.

We may also detach verses 15-19, since (a) the story is introduced by the statement that the angel spoke "a second time," which also is an editorial technique for linking stories (1 Kgs 9:2; Jer 1:13; 13:3); and (b) these verses have a different concern from that of 1-14—only

[8]Buttrick, *Interpreter's Bible,* vol. 1, p. 616.
[9]Sleeth, *Proclamation,* Series C, "Pentecost I" (1974), p. 54.

here are the events of those earlier verses connected with God's promise of a future for Abraham.

Who were the editors of this story? In terms of assignment to one of the sources, this story is difficult. On one hand, it seems to be E, since the word "God" (*'elohim)* is used for the deity (vv 1, 3, 8, 9, 12). On the other hand, the designation "the Lord" (Yahweh) is mentioned (v 11). Either this is an instance of the freedom of the sources to vary slightly in such usage, or it is evidence that the story has been reworked by later editors who used "Yahweh" terminology. The latter seems plausible, in view of the addition of J material in verses 15-19. In any case, we are dealing with the early collections (JE) and not the later (DP).

What was the situation at the time the text took its final shape? If the basic story line is from the E-source, then we should not be surprised that it stresses testing and obedience, a theme that has been mentioned previously as characteristic of this source and of the prophets during the late monarchical period.[10]

What questions does the text try to answer? That is most difficult, and much debated. It has been suggested that the story is a polemic against child sacrifice as Israel encountered it in the Land of Canaan, and as elements in Israel occasionally practiced it (2 Kgs 23:10; Jer 32:35). In this interpretation, God would be supplying an animal substitute and suggesting that this is to be the case hereafter. However, if that was the message of the story at some stage of its transmission, it is not very explicit in its present wording.

Other interpreters have suggested that the story

---

[10]See esp. Terry Fretheim, "The Jacob Traditions," *Interpretation* 26(1972):419ff.

began as a folk-explanation for a well-known place:
There is a sacred site whose name means "The Lord will
provide" because God provided a sacrificial animal for
Abraham (vv 8, 14). Presumably the place the story has
in mind is Moriah (v 2), a word seemingly related to the
word "provide" *(ra'ah)*. But if that were the original
purpose of the story, it has receded into the background.
The theme of "testing" has moved to the fore, and it is
one found elsewhere in Scripture.

How is the story related to its larger context? The
addition of verses 15-19 shifts the focus entirely. Now
the story is connected with the theme of God's promise
of offspring, and thus it is linked to the larger patriarchal
story. The Isaac of whom we read is Abraham's "only
son" (v 16), promised long before (12:7; 13:15-16),
delayed in arriving (15:2), and one his parents had
thought would never be born (17:17; 18:12). We thus see
that it is no ordinary parent who ponders the fate of his
child: The whole future of an Israel, of a Believing
Community, is at stake. The earlier theme of testing and
obedience now takes on ultimate importance. God now
seems to contradict himself, and the father of the faith
must choose wherein the future lies.

Assumptions in the Move from Past to Present

● A text may have more than one meaning, and I have
outlined two: the meaning of the author in the overall
literary unit (vv 1-14) (ch 3, I, C) and the meaning of the
story in its larger context (vv 1-19) (ch 3, V).
● I need not make a choice between meanings, as if
only one could be "right" and the others were "wrong."
Each addressed the community at a stage of its history
and each may make a contribution to the community's
self-understanding in the present (ch 2, III, E).

• Abraham's struggle concerns the future of Israel. Thus we must understand it in that fashion in the present, rather than draw moral lessons for our individual lives (ch 2, IV, C).

A Suggested Direction in the Present

I limit myself here to the larger meaning outlined above (vv 1-19). What is the Believing Community (Church or Synagogue, either at the national or local level) to do when a conflict develops between obedience to what is perceived to be the will of God in a given crisis, and a decision that may be detrimental to the organization in the long run? A given course of action may appear to be just and in accordance with the traditional teachings of the faith, and yet may encounter such opposition that the future of the entire community may be undermined. What are the leaders to do when, in the execution of what they perceive to be the traditional ideals, a large segment of the community threatens to "cut off the funds"? What are pastors to do when they realize that a loving and candid statement of the gospel will alienate part of, if not all the congregation? What were the executives of the United Presbyterian Church in the U.S.A. to do when they discussed financial support for Marxist Angela Davis, knowing that it might well cause numbers of persons to leave the church? Such moments are indeed a "test," and they determine wherein one's hope lies: Is it in God's power to do the impossible, or is it in maintaining the organization?

Possible False Directions

1. "How could Abraham know what God wanted him to do? How can we know?" A crucial question,

indeed! And the community must ponder it, not trusting individual judgment. Nonetheless, this is a question the text does not ask. We must at least listen to the text's question, before we turn to our own.

2. "Abraham was a good father, and we should try to imitate him: He demonstrated his faith for his child to see." Whatever Abraham's merits as a father, it must be added that such a message was not intended by the story's formulators and transmitters. As far as the various levels of meaning are concerned, it suffices only as "What the text means to the modern reader" (ch 3, IX). From my point of view, one should not begin by drawing moral lessons, as opposed to seeking the underlying theology (ch 2, IV, B). This is a story more about God than about Abraham. Furthermore, this story is about the future of Israel, and to see Abraham as the model father is to individualize it (ch 2, IV, C).

V. The Ten Commandments—Exodus 20:1-17

Background Information

Who were the editors of this story? Few passages in the Bible present more difficulties for that question than does this text. It has been assigned to E and to P, or thought to have D and P expansions of a basic E account.[11] In the face of such uncertainty, it is precarious to try to relate the text to specific historical circumstances. It is apparent, however, that the material has grown over the generations: (a) There are several versions of the Commandments (Exod 20; Exod 34; Deut 5), and they differ in greater and lesser detail; (b) God sometimes speaks in the first person (e.g., "I am

[11]See "Ten Commandments," *IDB, IDBS.*

the Lord your God"—v 6) and sometimes speaks of himself in the third person (e.g., "You shall not take the name of the Lord your God in vain"—v 7); (c) The commandments vary considerably in length, and there is some reason to believe that the longer forms often involve expansions. Since the series lacks any hint of life as it would have been lived in Canaan, it is not impossible that it had its beginnings in the wilderness prior to arrival in the promised land.[12]

What is its literary form? It is possible that this expression of the covenant between Israel and Yahweh was modeled after political treaties enacted by international powers. Recently discovered texts (suzerainty texts) describe the relationship between Hittite kings in the thirteenth century B.C. and their vassals (small nearby states). These treaty texts follow a set pattern: identification of the great king who offers relationship to the smaller states; a review of previous gracious acts; the obligations of the smaller states in view of what the great king already has done; provision for public reading of the treaty document; a list of witnesses to the signing of the treaty; and the blessings or curses which will befall the loyal or the traitor. The first three parts may be discoverable in Exodus 20: The great king identifies himself (v 2a), reviews previous gracious acts (v 2b), and states the obligations (Commandments) which the smaller treaty-members (Israelites) must obey (vv 3-17).

This political model and literary form sheds considerable light upon the motivation for obedience to the

---

[12]Other guidelines set at Sinai do betray a later origin. Thus Israelites own slaves (Exod. 21:2-11); live in dwellings with a doorpost (21:5); own cattle (21:28-32), which probably would not survive in the desert; cultivate fields and vineyards (22:5); etc.

Commandments, as ancient Israel may have understood it. Rather than assume that Israel was invited to keep the Commandments with a promise of reward if they will do so, it is important to realize that Israel already has received undeserved blessing. She was delivered from Egypt through no merit of her own. And how is one to respond to this gracious action on God's part? It must involve more than an emotional feeling, more than rational perception. To remember, as Israel understood it, is to act on the basis of the memory. And thus our text means, "I brought you up out of the land of Egypt: *therefore* do the following." We are given the authentic theological basis for ethics. Thus the Commandments are not legalisms, but concrete guidelines for the expression of gratitude; they are not "law," but responses to the gospel. As it later would be expressed, "We love, because he first loved us" (1 John 4:19).

How is the story related to its larger context? Chapters 1–19 tell the full story of Israel's enslavement in Egypt, the escape through the miraculous intervention of the Lord, the survival in the wilderness, and the arrival at the sacred mountain, which the preface to our text compresses into a single phrase, ". . . brought you out of the land of Egypt." These chapters reinforce the proposal that the Commandments are responses to God, rather than self-sufficient legalisms to be obeyed simply because God commands it or because they exemplify the way "decent" people act (ch 1, I, A).

Assumptions in the Move from Past to Present

● It is important to consider the meaning of an entire literary unit (ch 3, I, C). Here, however, we must make a distinction between a collection of ethical guidelines and the narratives discussed previously. Each guideline does have an existence of its own; sentences in the previous narratives only contribute to a larger whole. But this collection of guidelines has an overall principle that could be overlooked if we were to concentrate upon one or another of the individual commandments. Only when we recognize the divine action which ought to engender gratitude, should we go on to the specific suggestions for its expression (ch 2, IV, B).

• The Commandments are addressed to collective Israel, although of necessity, they can affect only individuals. Nonetheless, the "you" of the text has a wider application than the individual reader in the present (ch 2, IV, C; ch 3, II). Thus what God has done for "me" is to be set in the context of what has been done for "us."

A Suggested Direction in the Present

Israel, standing at Mt. Sinai, was reminded that it owed its collective existence to an undeserved action of the deity. The community thus created was a source of life to those who would join it. It still survives, however modified, in two daughter religions, Judaism and Christianity. Although the Church and Synagogue in the present did not participate directly in those ancient events, they nonetheless owe their existence to them and still transmit ancient Israel's life-giving power. Although the Church sometimes may fail in its mission, there are those who will attest that it transmits spiritual life, if not psychological, social, economic, and sometimes even physical life. Thus when the story of its founding is retold (i.e., when Exod 1–19 is read), we may remember anew our dependence, our gratitude to God (Exod 20:1-11), and our responsibility for others within the community (20:12-17). The text, then, is a thanksgiving for the founding of the community, a thanksgiving that is translated into concrete action.

Possible False Directions

1. "Focus upon an individual Commandment." While this is certainly defensible, certain dangers must be pointed out. (a) We may be tempted to select a Commandment that we perceive others to be violating but one that will leave us untouched. For example, it may be more comfortable for the pastor to condemn Sabbath-violators than to discuss idolatry, which surely would condemn the pastor as well (ch 2, II, C). (b) There may be a tendency to concentrate upon the negative commandments. Condemnation seems to be easier than encouragement. In any case, it is well to remember that the basic function of this material is not to condemn, but to aid in the expression of the gospel. (c) The Commandments are not arranged into categories of bad, worse, and worst, as far as violation is concerned. Such a ranking may exist in the mind of the community or its leaders, but it does not take its clue from the text itself. Consequently, persons may be shocked at theft, or murder, or adultery, but scarcely lift an eyebrow at disrespect for parents ("Let's put them in a nursing home so they won't inconvenience us!") or neglect of Sabbath worship ("Let's go to the beach Sunday morning!").

More serious is the possibility that, in focusing upon a single Commandment, the overall motivation for obedience would be neglected.

2. "We all have something to be grateful to God for!" However, this text does not call for gratitude in general, but for a specific act of physical deliverance of a

community wherein we still participate. We must be careful not to move prematurely to individualize and spiritualize the saving act (ch 2, IV, C; D).

3. "God will destroy America because we are breaking the Ten Commandments!" Note, however, that the Commandments are positive expressions of gratitude, more than legalisms meant to threaten or to result in punishment. Indeed, no threat is mentioned in the text. Furthermore, Israel deliberately accepted the covenant relationship as her response to God, and hence condemnation would result if that relationship were broken. But America is a modern secular state whose guiding "story" is not the Bible, but the Constitution and the United States civil code (neither of which, incidentally, mention "God"). How can a group be judged for breaking that which it did not accept in the first place? The name "Israel" in the Bible cannot be exchanged easily for that of any group in the present that tends to offend the ethical sensibilities of the interpreter (ch 2, IV, E; III, B).

VI. The Necessity for Tassels on Garments— Numbers 15:37-41

Background Information

Who were the editors of this story? This small story, like the rest of the chapter, is usually attributed to the P-source. Note the concern with sacrificial procedure (vv 1-31), sabbath violation (vv 32-36), and characteristic language (e.g., "throughout their generations," v 38). Nonetheless, it is a separate, perhaps once-independent story, set apart by content, by an introductory formula ("The Lord said . . ."), and a standard closing formula

("I am the Lord your God"). Its stress on holiness (v 40) relates it to other stories (Lev 17–26 in particular) sometimes called the Holiness Code (H)—apparently a collection of materials used by the Priestly Editors.[13]

What was the situation at the time the text took its final shape? Israel's struggle to maintain her identity during the Exile and early post-exilic age has been discussed previously. In view of the needs of that age, it is not surprising to find the P-source preserving a story which stresses the need for concrete reminders that one belongs to a community whose gratitude to God is to be expressed in terms of obedience.

How is the situation addressed? Whereas some traditional ways of "remembering" have been taken away (country, monarchy, temple, festivals), there are others that cannot so easily be removed from the exiles' sight. Just as their sabbath may be observed not only in Palestine, but everywhere, so a particular item of clothing can be worn wherever one goes.

How is the story related to its larger context? Three once-independent stories have been combined. First, the people are encouraged to remember that they have been chosen by God and are to observe special values and norms, but it is also confessed that lapses of memory are possible, given human nature (vv 22-31). This likelihood is illustrated by the story of a man who gathers wood for a fire on the sabbath day (vv 32-36). Then follows our text, giving a concrete means whereby such an event might be avoided (vv 37-41).

How has earlier custom been modified? Tassels on the edges of garments are widely attested in the Ancient

[13]See "Pentateuch" and "Leviticus," *IDB.*

Near East and may have been connected with magic, or perhaps served only as decoration. Now they are given a new purpose as reminders of one's identity. The original purpose of the blue thread can no longer be recovered, but it now serves to remind one of the community to which one belongs. Later, the rabbis will be more explicit: It is to be blue because blue is the color of the sky, and the sky reminds us of God.

Assumptions in the Move from Past to Present

● Although this passage may appear to be irrelevant for life in the present, the fact that it is Scripture demands a careful hearing (ch 2, III, B).

● Behind the mere statement of an ancient fashion in dress is a deeper reason for the story's preservation. What was at stake for survival, for identity, when this story was remembered? (ch 2, III, C).

● The identity-crisis of the ancient Israelites was not unique to them. The difficulty in remembering "who we are" transcends time and place. The human condition under the covenant, past and present, has considerable similarity (ch 2, III, B). Our text has endured because it proposed a workable solution to a difficult and perennial condition of the believer.

● In our day, the author's intention may be met without necessarily following the "letter" of his guidelines. The application today may take a different form, and yet the "spirit" can remain the same (ch 3, III).

A Suggested Direction in the Present

Our tendency toward faithlessness may not entirely be the result of a will to disobey. A contributing factor is that we lack concrete reminders of our membership in the covenant community. Sadly, the Church is moving away from insistance upon tangible aids. The Roman

Catholic Church once prescribed a special diet for Friday, but now has abandoned the practice. Protestants, on the other hand, usually have frowned upon such alleged superstitions as St. Christopher's medals, thinking themselves too mature spiritually to need them. But it is the Protestant, above all others, whose life reflects a failure to remember.

Whether we revive the practice of wearing tassels (as a biblical "literalist" should), or observe other traditional reminders, or devise some new means of assistance, is relatively unimportant. What is indispensable is that the need for reminders be recognized and implemented, perhaps after discussion in the community (ch 2, III, B).

AIDS FOR THE INTERPRETER

I. General Works

The Interpreter's Dictionary of the Bible (IDB). 4 vols. Ed. George Buttrick (Nashville: Abingdon Press, 1962), with a *Supplementary Volume (IDBS)*. Gen. ed. Keith Crim (1976). Easily the most comprehensive general aid for the study of Scripture, with articles on individual biblical books, persons-places-things, and methods of interpretation. Specifically, the following articles will supplement my discussion: *IDB*—Deuteronomy; Legend; Literature; Versions; *IDBS*—Deuteronomic History; Deuteronomy; Elohist; Etiology; Genesis; Gloss; Homosexuality; *Lex Talionis;* Poetry; Priestly Writers; Promise to the Patriarchs; Text, Hebrew, History of; Textual Criticism; Tradition Criticism; Yahwist.

Barr, James. *The Bible in the Modern World* (New York: Harper & Row, 1973). After discussing such concepts as "inspiration" and "authority," the author turns to the problems cultural relativism creates for us as we interpret Scripture.

Best, Ernest. *From Text to Sermon: Responsible Use of the New Testament in Preaching* (Atlanta: John Knox

Press, 1978). Although based upon the NT text, the points the author makes are transferable to use in the OT. Contains a discussion and evaluation of such traditional techniques for contemporization as parallelism, demythologization, substitution, generalization, etc. The book is less helpful with positive suggestions.

Keck, Leander E. *The Bible in the Pulpit: The Renewal of Biblical Preaching* (Nashville: Abingdon, 1978).

Sanders, James. *God Has a Story, Too* (Philadelphia: Fortress Press, 1979). Several excellent sermons, with a commentary on how they evolved from the biblical text in view of specific congregational needs. The preface is an expanded version of "Hermeneutics," *IDBS*.

II. Commentaries

The Interpreter's One-Volume Commentary on the Bible. Ed. Charles M. Laymon (Nashville: Abingdon, 1971). General articles, plus commentary on each biblical book.

Proclamation Commentaries: Old Testament Witnesses for Preaching Series (Philadelphia: Fortress Press). *Genesis–Numbers* was written by Foster McCurley (1979); *Deuteronomy* and *Jeremiah* by Elizabeth Achtemeier (1978). Generally a competent treatment of themes, with concentration upon what the text meant (as opposed to what it may mean now).

The Old Testament Library Series (Philadelphia: Westminster Press), especially volumes *Genesis* (Gerhard von Rad, 1961) and *Exodus* (Brevard Childs, 1974).